What your *Father* should have told You

wise words for today's woman

What your *Father* should have told You

wise words for today's woman

TERRENCE AUTRY

What Your Father Should Have Told You: Wise Words for Today's Woman by Terrence Autry

Cover Design by Tonya Neal
Interior Design by Adina Cucicov

© Copyright 2019

First Printing, 2019

ISBN: 9781072402367

Printed in the U.S.A.

Table of Contents

Introduction..vii

Chapter 1 Yes, you are more than enough................................1

Chapter 2 Yes, you are beautiful.....................................21

Chapter 3 Yes, you need a father's eye..............................45

Chapter 4 Yes, sex is always on his mind............................67

Chapter 5 Yes, you have an issue....................................85

Chapter 6 Yes, this will hurt you..................................107

Chapter 7 Yes, you need to know when He is ready...................129

Chapter 8 Yes, you always will need your *Heavenly* Father........149

Epilogue..167

Introduction

"You are altogether beautiful, my darling;
there is no flaw in you."
~ Song of Solomon 4:7 ~

L et me begin by saying, I have no daughters. Instead, I have two wonderful adult sons, both of whom have been a great joy and blessing to both my wife and myself. I have tried my best to teach them the meaning of manhood—responsibility, integrity, respect for women and family, and a personal walk with God. I have given them my share of "father and sons" talks; a series of open conversations about mature, God-honoring manhood. We have discussed spiritual life, adulthood, family, women, sex, addictions, and money—all of which, I believe, point to the character and quality of a man. I used these talks to prepare my sons for the most responsible manhood possible. Though there are many other things I wish I had shared, I do believe God has used these talks to help them both become good mature men. My wife and I could not be prouder.

Therefore, I admit at the onset that I *never* have fathered a daughter. I never have raised one. I know nothing about braided hair or finger nail polish. I never have attended cheerleading practices, or wiped tears due to friendship betrayals. I confess that I do not know the first thing about raising daughters into women of dignity. So, why am I writing a father/daughter book?

As a Pastor, I have been ushered into the unenviable position of spiritual fatherhood for many women in the church and community I serve. I have witnessed the carnage of hurt, trauma, and pain many women have endured. I have encouraged women through domestic abuse, sexual assault, betrayal, abandonment, poor relationship choices, loneliness, and low self-esteem. At times, the task seemed insurmountable and beyond restoration. I, however, had been given a window into the world of hurting women. The hurt was strikingly similar to the grief of Rachel in the Scriptures,

> "A voice was heard in Ramah, weeping and loud lamentation, Rachel weeping for her children; she refused to be comforted, because they are no more." (Matthew 2:18, ESV)

Like Rachel, I heard many women weep in agony, refusing comfort because of the depth of their pain.

Surprisingly, however, I found that simple fatherly advice gave women immense comfort and hope for their difficulties. Buried under the rubble of hurt was an innocent daughter, longing for her father's voice that could inspire the dawn of a new day. I quickly discovered that just as my sons needed father/son advice, many women needed similar counsel to find refuge, stability, and direction for their lives. Though mothers are absolutely foundational to the rearing and nurturing of any daughter, fathers in no way are incidental. I believe God put something in a father that lifts a woman's spirit, builds her self-esteem, and reinvigorates her confidence.

Therefore, I wrote this book for women—to give them a fatherly perspective. In this book, I share the invaluable principles that have helped many women "live again" by working through their pain and difficulty. There is something about a father's presence and voice that is therapeutic for a daughter.

My wife is a very strong, confident woman. She would be the first to say that she is not perfect on any scale, yet carries herself with a sense of purpose, dignity and incredible confidence. Much of her confidence came from her strong, progressive-thinking, mother. She gave Lisa a glorious and grand vision of womanhood to emulate. Lisa also gained confidence from her late father. At the age of 12, when most young girls are ripening into womanhood,

Lisa lost her father. Though traumatic and life-altering, Lisa retained many treasures her father instilled in her.

For example, Lisa recalls how her father routinely serenaded her to a piano tune entitled, "Beautiful Brown Eyes." She remembers sitting with her father on the piano bench as he played and crooned this beautiful ballad just for her.

Can you imagine what that must have felt like? Can you imagine how that must have boosted Lisa's confidence at a tender age? Can you sense the lasting impact a father serenading his daughter can have long term? Lisa's father influenced her confidence for a life time. If Lisa's mother put the cream in her coffee, then surely her father was a hefty dose of sugar.

I believe every woman needs a similar example. Mothers always will be indispensable. Fathers, however, bring a unique voice of affirmation; a slightly different yet important perspective to the challenging needs of an evolving woman.

The importance of fatherly advice for women became even more apparent to me during a recent discussion in our church. We had a series of lessons and discussions with women about the role of fathers in a womans life. We would learn that about 80% of the women present either did not have a father in the home or simply received little to no advice from their father during their adolescent or adult years. Furthermore, though many appreciated the amazing responsibility their mothers carried in rearing them, they found that the absence of their father greatly affected how they felt about themselves and how they handled their romantic relationships. Finally, to my surprise, many women found tremendous relief in connecting their hurts to the advice shared that will be covered in this book.

For too long, we have made the false assumption that sons need fathers more than daughters. Sons always will need their father, and I continue to do everything possible to be available for my own sons. However, too many women live without fatherly advice that may inspire the confidence they need to discover their purpose for living. Too many women are stuck in a cycle of relationship mistakes because they just do not know how to detect deceptive advances. More importantly, many women struggle with their sense of self that require the care and affirmation of a loving father. This book provides fatherly advice that every young girl, teenager, and adult woman needs.

The book is designed around a fictional story and character about a young lady named Gianna. Gianna, unfortunately, experiences a devastating breakup with her boyfriend, and consequently, seeks counsel from her Pastor. In these sessions, she eventually discovers that the breakup revealed something deeper. The breakup opened a door of learning about life, herself, and her need for a father. It is an amazing journey of self-discovery, renewed confidence and a deeper faith. She emerges from her betrayal as a maturing and growing woman—not perfect by a long shot, but far better prepared to handle life and future relationships. She learns how to handle life with some good fatherly advice.

At the close of each chapter, there are discussion questions to assist the reader in working through the lessons and principles presented in the narrative. My hope is that this story will inspire you to self-discovery, personal growth, and purposeful living.

If you have wondered about the absence of a father, and its effect on your relationship choices, then this book is for you. It will help you navigate the landscape of love with a fresh perspective—what your father should have told you. If you have a father, but would like to deepen your relationship with him regarding the challenges you face, then this book is for the both of you. If you have a father, but do not have the kind of relationship you need with him, I hope this book will bridge a stronger relationship for the both of you. In no way am I undermining the importance of his role and voice in your life. Many times, as fathers, we simply do not know how to advise daughters. I believe this book will help the both of you learn together.

Lastly and possibly most important, this book is for fathers with daughters. If you are a father and want to encourage your daughter, my prayer is that you and your daughter will read this book together and talk about the advice your daughter is longing to hear from you. She needs you more than you may know. You need her, too. I pray God will bless you both.

Chapter 1

Yes, you are more than enough

"The hunger for love is much more difficult to remove than the hunger for bread."
~ Mother Teresa ~

"I can't believe it happened, again," Gianna exclaimed as she wiped away her streaming tears. "It just keeps happening to me, over and over. Another break up. And I really thought this was the one. Tired of being the star in the same old miserable movie. Is something wrong with me?"

One word popped into my mind as I sat and listened to Gianna's story—heartbreaks. There is no way around them. We all have them. We can educate ourselves; we can put in the relationship work; we can learn from relationship gurus (though I sometime have my doubts about these 'gurus'). We can even hype ourselves with inspiring slogans—"what doesn't kill me makes me stronger" or "never again." Yet, life has an alarming sinister twist, paving a path to the very thing we try so hard to avoid.

"I should have known something was up," Gianna continued. "He always found a way to blame me for his issues. 'You always see your side. What about my side? You don't know how hard it is on a man,'" Gianna said, mimicking his tone and mannerisms. "Where did that get me? 'Try to be understanding,' I told myself. It's just so hard to detect what is really under the hood of anyone anymore. I mean, we all have a few dents, right? I'm just tired of this $#%#@. Shouldn't this be easier?"

Like an ostrich, Gianna buried her head in her hands as she wept, softly. Though ostriches bury their heads in holes to create safe havens for their young, we do it because the truth hurts. I gently pushed the tissue box toward her as the ones in her hands had died a shriveled death. An interesting image, I thought. It may capture what Gianna felt—a shriveling death, one with an irreversible end. But I knew better. If the grave couldn't hold Jesus, then surely heartache would never have the last word.

I am not your typical Pastor. I questioned my calling for half my ministry because I was not standard clergy—black suit, white collar, cuff links, preacher hat, or erudite speech—just not my thing. I do, however, love a good inspirational hoop. I had to really trust God that it was okay to be different as a Pastor. I still have my struggles though. Thus, my members know that they can share freely. "Put it all on the table," I tell them. "Hold back nothing"—blood, mess, filth and yes, the profanity. Cleanse your heart. If it is okay to cleanse a colon from time to time, what harm is there to cleanse our souls of the infection of a heartbreak?

"Get it all out of your system Gianna." I said. "Trust me, even after you find the right one, it is still harder to make it work. You know I have often said to the congregation, 'relationships are just like playing football...'"

"...I know, I know Pastor. 'You can't expect to play the game and not get hurt.' I'm just tired of the game! There has to be an easier way. *And why does it ever have to be a game?*"

Gianna's last question demanded to be felt. Her pain was quickly coming of age. It too wanted affirmation. I have watched and prayed for many people that have endured unmitigated agony due to a horrible health condition or illness—broken bones, traction recovery, inexplicable and persistent migraines, amputations, and even cancer. In time, pain makes itself known. It will not sit silently by. Pain has its own voice and Gianna's was clearly serving notice that she was here.

"It is a game that is not always fair," I replied. "There are shifting ground rules in all relationships, which is why we get hurt. The good news, however, is that you have people who care for you. And like all storms, this too will pass."

"Pastor, why does this keep happening to me? Am I just plain stupid?"

"Of course not!" I shot back. "Gianna, this is your first challenge at overcoming heartache. Learn when your pain is talking. It has its own voice, and it is talking to you now. It demands your attention and will indoctrinate you with 'false news.' Like a snake, you have to cut it off at the head or else it will poison your thinking. What happened to you could have happened to anybody. It has happened to all of us. No one is immune. You're not blind; you are not an idiot; and for God's sake, you are not stupid! That is your pain talking. Your next step is to grow deaf ears to the voice of your pain."

"Then, why does this keep happening to me, Pastor?"

The sincerity in Gianna's eyes was unmistakable. She needed to hear the truth for herself; but not today. She was not ready. She still thought an answer will soften her pain. It never does. Answers have never healed a single hurt. Knowing why a child molester destroys the life of an innocent child, does not resolve the agony of the mother or the child. Only time, the gracious hand of God, and a patient professional ear *may* help us move past pain. Even then, there are no guarantees. We live in a broken and evil world, in which pain and evil are the norm. Sadly, it takes catastrophic pain to wake us to this truth.

"Why don't you tell me what happened?" I gently asked.

"Pastor, don't change the subject on me," Gianna responded somewhat defensively. "I know you. Grew up in this church. Love my church. I know you care for me and my family. I came because I knew you cared. But I need to know for myself. I know there is a lesson in all this. So, spare me the pastoral touchy feely garbage! I can take it. We Johnsons ain't punks!"

"No, Johnsons are not punks by a long shot!" I said, trying to restrain my laughter. Thank God Gianna was smiling, now.

"You are not going to let this go, are you?" I asked.

Gianna sat with her arms folded in protest, while staring at me through her dried tears.

"Okay. Let's start with the most important issue in any relationship."

Leaning forward on my desk and looking her squarely into the eyes, I said, "You!"

"Me?"

"Yes you," I replied, "not in the sense that you are at fault or an idiot. And *pleeease* do not ever use the word 'stupid' again! Instead, you are on the right track that there is a lesson to be learned. Indie sings a song that has a great lyric that says, 'It is the ones who are close to you that hurt you the most.' Maybe it hurts so much because we love so hard, sometimes *too hard*. There is nothing wrong with loving hard. Jesus loves hard. But sometimes, we love hard with an expectation. We say to ourselves, 'since I am giving you all this good loving, I ought to get something in return,' as if we can guarantee love. Sounds more like a transaction, a business arrangement. Where is the soul in that?

Though our intentions are sincere, we really are negotiating the terms of the relationship for our interests.

Unfortunately, love does not work that way. You can't transact love. I get that no one wants to play the fool. Consequently, we do everything we can to protect ourselves. There is plain common sense in that. On the other hand, loving with your guard up doesn't feel good, does it? Love that is really love must always be freely given."

"Makes sense. But what is the lesson, Pastor?" Gianna pressed.

"God never loves transactionally," I said. "God never loves with his guard up. God chooses to love us freely. God loves us without restraint, knowing full well that we will hurt him. He loves us with the fierceness of a tiger and yet grants us the freedom of an eagle. 'You want to fly away after I have given you all this good loving? Go right ahead,' God says. 'But know this: I loved you like no other. You will never find a love like mine,' God says to us. That is true love—thoroughly unconditional. There is nothing like it."

"I know that Pastor, but what does that have to do with me? And how does that help me in the future? Tired of this crap. He did the dirt anyway!"

"Here's how," I responded. "God's love reminds us that *we are more than enough.* When we love others in exchange for acceptance and affirmation, we are setting ourselves up for a major disappointment. People, by nature, will hurt you—even the ones with the best intentions. Moreover, even if the people we love did accept and affirm us, it usually falls far short of the love we need. We become disappointed, we gripe, even feel insulted, to only be left with a deeper dissatisfaction.

That is why we need acceptance long before we love others. We need to know we are already valued. We need to know we are already affirmed and cherished. We need love from another world. Though this world may turn its back on us, God gives us love from another world that is forever."

"Sounds good Pastor, but I already know I am more than enough. Like I said, Johnsons ain't punks!"

"Don't remind me. Did you see signs that something was awry?" I asked.

"Yes."

"Why didn't you walk?" I asked.

"Because I thought I needed to give more. Give it more time, I told myself," Gianna said with confidence.

"No, you thought you *weren't* more than enough. So you gave more of yourself to prove to him that you were *more than enough* when you already were more than enough. That is a transaction," I said.

Gianna paused and stared. No words. I learned that long pauses mean the truth has hit home. Gianna knew it was true.

"That might be true, Pastor. Maybe that is why I love hard. Can't fault me for that. If love is real love, it ought to be to the full, right?"

"Of course. But you have to love hard for the right reasons. Are you loving hard for acceptance? Or are you loving hard because you are already accepted? There is a difference," I said.

"How does God help me with this hurt?" Gianna asked, changing the subject.

"*Process*," I said. "As my grandmother was so fond of saying, 'this too shall pass.' Just like wounds to the body need time to heal, we do too. In the meantime, let the wound drive you to God's loving arms where you can know *you are more than enough*.

"Okay Pastor. It is not even Sunday morning, but I need this."

Rachel—Value and Purpose

"Got your notes ready? You know there are some lessons to learn, right?" I asked.

"Pastor, I am in no mood for notetaking today," Gianna stated.

"You said you wanted to learn the lesson? Or did I mishear you? Johnsons ain't no punk, remember?"

Smiling, Gianna said, "Let's do this."

"Okay. Today, we're going to look at the life of Rachel in Genesis 29 and talk about what it means to know you are more than enough. This is critical to your sense of self, and critical to lasting relationships. In fact, this truth may be the single difference between great and mediocre relationships.

I'll tell you something else. Men gravitate toward an 'I'm more than enough' woman than any other type of woman, if they are interested in a serious relationship. If he senses that she feels she is an 'I'm not good enough' woman—unsure of herself, doubting her decisions, assaulting her own self-worth and the worth of others—he simply will not waste his time. Contrary to popular opinion, a man wants a woman with confidence.

"Pastor, I'm not with you on that," Gianna quickly interjected. "If that's the case, why are brothers always chasing these crazy high-maintenance chicks? I'm not feeling that at all. Besides, Floyd was a little rattled when I expressed my opinions. Men don't want strong women; even when they say they want a serious relationship."

"Why would you want a man that chases that type of woman, anyway?" I asked. "An 'I'm more than enough' woman is confident: nothing like these crazy high-maintenance women. She doesn't need to *check* her man or *argue* every detail. She's not arrogant, loud, or saucy. Granted, she's not a door mat either. She has her own thoughts and opinions. She's never afraid to express them. She, however, expresses them with confidence and civility. She is rarely rattled; at least she doesn't show it. She doesn't apologize for her views because her views are hers; end of story. Trust me, a brother wants a confident woman, not an insecure woman."

Seeing that Gianna seemed receptive to what I said, I continued. "Most men lose their stomachs with compliant women. They would rather not be bothered. Sadly, more women would have a good man if they turned the volume down on their tone, and turned up the volume on their convictions! Men walk away from that mess.

Women, on the other hand, will complain, gripe, scream, and yet stay. Why do you think women do that, Gianna?

"No answer, Pastor. Makes no sense; but we do it," Gianna replied.

"I'll tell you why—back to my original point: women don't believe they're more than enough. There comes a point, Gianna, that you must choose to live life from a place of deep conviction and not convenience. Convenience will get you played. Convictions and values will keep you sane, and true to yourself, and what people respect."

Gianna had a thoughtful expression on her face. She said, "okay Pastor. You got me thinking."

I asked, "Can I keep going?" She nodded her assent.

"The right man," I said, "will love you because of your conviction that you are more than enough and expect to be treated as such. That's not arrogance; it's confidence, an assurance that comes from our Maker. It simply says: Respect my value and it's not up for debate!"

"Furthermore," I continued, "there's an important distinction between men and women. Men are goal-oriented. That is, we need a challenge, a goal. Even if it is the *wrong goal,* we will pour all our energies into it. We shoot for a target. We may miss, but at least we had a target. It's never the thrill of the hunt that excites a man; it's the thrill of the catch. This is why men chase the most challenging women; not because he loves the chase, but because he loves challenge. Can he win her heart? That's the goal. I know that's crude, but it's central to the psychology of men.

Don't ever be his goal; make sure he has conquered his goals when he meets you. If his sights are set on conquering you, he will probably never love you. But if he has conquered purposeful goals or is even in the process of seriously, and I do mean seriously, conquering his goals, then he is more likely ready for a companion."

"Wow! I never thought of it like that," Gianna said. "Floyd had his goals, but in hindsight, he really struggled to stay focused. I guess that should have been my first clue."

"Maybe so," I responded. "It's definitely something to think about in the future. So, that's men. In contrast, women typically are relational, meaning emotions are paramount for women. Unfortunately, emotions are like the waves of the sea—calm one minute, choppy the next. So, one minute, women are confident, feeling good, aggressive, ready to conquer new worlds. The next minute: depressed, doubting, wondering, 'Am I smart enough? Am I pretty enough? Am I cute enough? Am I dressed well enough? Am I...'"

"Am I loving enough? Am I caring enough? Am I *fineee* enough?" Gianna interrupted.

"You got it! Women drench themselves with a deluge of doubting questions that drive them to emotional insanity! You become like fish, flopping back and forth on a deck of a boat, not sure where to land. Each question of doubt points to one nagging, yet simple question, 'Am I enough?' Many times, women know in their heads they're enough; but their hearts refuse to concur. Nine times out of ten, if a woman fell for a knucklehead, it was because this question was the unruly toddler, straining on her love nerve—Am I enough? She knew she was, but just wouldn't accept it," I said.

"So true," Gianna said, shaking her head in concurrence.

"Make no mistake," I continued. "This same question haunted Rachel, but she had a father who helped her tame it. Trust me, this question never goes away. It can hibernate for a season. It may retreat to an exile, leading you to think the war is over. Eventually, however, it'll stalk you like a thief, waiting to steal your confidence and wipe out your self-esteem.

Let's shift gears, now to where I've been trying to go. This is where a father is so important to a daughter's sense of self. A good father helps tame the 'Am I enough' questions that assaults his daughter's esteem. A good father reminds her over and over again, *you are more than enough*. He tells her numerous times a day, until she believes it without even thinking about it.

Look at Rachel's reaction upon meeting her love, Jacob,

"And Jacob told Rachel that he was her father's kinsman, and that he was Rebekah's son, and she ran and told her father." (Genesis 29:12, ESV)

I love this atypical love story of boy meets girl. Boy meets girl. Boy falls for girl. But don't miss the script flip—*girl doesn't fall for boy*—at least not yet. Girl, instead, runs home to dad! Why? Girl knows she's more than enough. Until dad approves of this boy, she's not going to fall for boy. That's what your father should have told you, over and over again, even into your adult years—you are more than enough.

"Definitely didn't get that," Gianna blurted out.

I continued. "Notice something else about her father,

"While he was still speaking with them, Rachel came with her father's sheep, for she was a shepherdess." (Genesis 29:9, ESV)

Dad made sure his daughter had a purpose. Long before she met Jacob, she was shepherding! How did Rachel quell the question, 'Am I enough?' Her daddy raised her in a purpose. 'You're more than enough,' he often told her. But to prove to her that she was more than enough, he mentored her in the family business of shepherding. The message? You have a life. You're a person all by yourself. You have a purpose. Her daddy instilled in her a sense of purpose that tamed the 'Am I enough' question."

"I knew I was getting away from my purpose. Should have listened to my first mind," Gianna commented.

"That's your pain talking. Stop doubting yourself. Better to have loved and missed, than to never have loved at all. Takes courage to love," I said.

"Shepherding," I continued, "was more than a job for a woman. If she was single, she worked for her father. If she was married, she worked for her husband. If she was unmarried, she worked for her father for the rest of her life."

"Ewww, that's no fun." Gianna said.

"I know, it was a different world," I said. "There were no other options for women then. Occasionally, she may have traveled to the local well to draw water, but even that was women's work.[1] The fact that Laban trained his daughter for the family business signifies how much he valued her. Her father believed in her. In essence, he wanted her to know, you are more than a wife. You are more than a mother. You are more than a boo! You are a woman, made in God's image, made for a fulfilling-purpose. You are more than enough. You with me so far?" I asked.

"Yeah, I am Pastor," Gianna responded. "I do have a tendency to invest more energy into my relationships rather than a worthy purpose. I guess I am still working my checklist—get the killer degree, killer career, killer house and car, and a fineee man to boot! I guess I need to ditch the list, huh?"

Laughing, I said, "You are such a trip. Not quite. Maybe a change in order. The key to the list is purpose. The late Myles Munroe may have stated it best regarding the importance of purpose, *"The greatest tragedy in life is not death, but a life without a purpose."*

---

1 Genesis 24:15-16.

"Deep, Pastor."

"Yes, Munroe was deep and profound," I concurred. "Gianna, I am so convinced that many people experience heartaches, frustrations, and emptiness, not because of bad relationships, *but because of no life-changing purpose.* By purpose, I mean a fulfilling mission that honors God and impacts people for good. When you influence people for good, you experience a feeling of significance and satisfaction. Furthermore, when you sense that this influence is from another world, you discover why you were placed on the earth. This is purpose. This is what makes life worth living. That great 21st century philosopher, Steve Harvey may have said it best, 'Career is what you are paid for, calling is what you are made for.'"

"I never thought of Steve Harvey as a philosopher," Gianna said, laughing.

Smiling, I said, "Wisdom comes from some of the most unlikely places."

"I want to close this session with something my wife keenly observed from the life of Deborah, the prophetess," I said.

"Lisa is the bomb! I want to hear this," Gianna exlaimed.

Shaking my head, I continued. "Judges Chapter 4 tells the story of a woman by the name of Deborah, a leader and a judge of the nation of Israel. God used her, mightily, to deliver his people from their oppressors. Who says God can't use a woman?"

"I know that is right," Gianna seconded.

"In this story," I continued, "Deborah's character serves as a model for women in leadership. Lisa, however, has pointed out, quite profoundly, that something of greater value might be overlooked about Deborah. Notice the order the text uses to describe Deborah,

"Now Deborah, a prophetess, the wife of Lappidoth, was judging Israel at that time." (Judges 4:4, ESV)

The text gives us five traits about Deborah—her name, her purpose, her marital status, her husband's name, and her career. Notice the order of the descriptions. Her purpose, which is a prophetess, precedes her identity as a wife or even her career as a judge. This text challenges us all to assess, how do we define ourselves? Today, too many women define themselves based on their love relationship or even their careers. Deborah, to the contrary, defined herself first and foremost by her purpose. She is poignantly clear on *whose she is*, God's daughter. She's, also clear on what God has called her to be, a prophetess. She knew she belonged to God and had a purpose from God before she belonged to her husband."

"I like that," Gianna said.

"When you know your purpose, you know you are far more than enough. I think Lisa is right on this one— Deborah was more than enough long before she met her husband. When we work in our purpose, as in the case of Deborah, we're confident, not cocky; we're strong, not

16

aggressive; we're prudent, not unsure of ourselves. We're God's children. We bear the deep conviction that we are more than enough. Can you imagine the reservoir of love Deborah had to offer her husband?" I asked.

"Moreover, I would add that Deborah had a broad vision of womanhood that was far ahead of its time for the ancient world. Again, womanhood in the ancient world was confined to three roles—wife, children, and homemaker. There were no other options. All these roles were at the behest of the father or husband. Deborah broadened her vision of womanhood to include a purpose from God and a career in the world.

Too many women carry an ancient worldview for relationships. That is, their entire value system is tethered to a husband and family. There is nothing wrong with wanting a husband and family, but in God's kingdom, women are more than wives and mothers. Women are more than companions and nurturers. Those are truly important roles for the stability of the family, however women also have value and purpose. They too, have a higher calling to impact the world. They, too, can experience a supernatural satisfaction of the soul. The clearest way I believe God helps us know that we're loved is through our kingdom purpose. All of God's children have a purpose, including God's daughters."

"So, if you were my daughter," I stated, "I would remind you every day of your life that you are more than enough. I would not have let a day go by without reminding you of that fact. Furthermore, I would have exposed you to numerous worthy endeavors for the discovery of your purpose. I would have reminded you that God called you to a purpose, long before Floyd or any other man. And it is God's purpose that helps you feel good about you. God's purpose helps you experience affirmation. God's purpose helps you *discover your passion;* and *know acceptance.* God's purpose will give you a reason for living. Then, you will find rest in your own skin. Yes, you are more than enough. And that is what your father should have told you," I said.

"Nope. My father never told me that," Gianna said.

Personal and Group Reflection Questions

1) What touched you most in this chapter? Make a list of what touched you in this chapter and then examine why.

_____

_____

_____

_____

_____

_____

_____

2) Can you relate to Gianna's experience? Explain.

_____

_____

_____

_____

_____

_____

_____

3) Do you feel 'more than enough?' Explain.

....

....

....

....

4) Are your relationships "transactional?" Explain. Is unconditional love in relationships possible?

....

....

....

....

5) Do you have a passion that points to a purpose? If so, what
are you passionate about? Before you read the next chapter,
make a list of three things you are passionate about. Then
develop deadlines for investigating these areas.

....

....

....

....

....

Chapter 2

Yes, you are beautiful

"A smile is the most beautiful curve
on a women's body."
~ Nicki Minaj ~

"You said Floyd was always blaming you for his issues?" I said, as I started our second session.

I was so glad Gianna stayed with it. Many rarely bother for a second session, thinking a good cry and a few wise words heal the hurt. Others, understandably, fear what the deeper hurt may reveal. It is a process, but a fruitful one.

Quick to speak, Gianna responded, "Well, Floyd was very flirtatious. I first thought that he was simply an outgoing social kind of guy. Besides, that is how I met him. I never would have had the nerve to talk to him after an outing at Top Golf. I am just not like that. Floyd can strike up a conversation with the Pope. Anyway, Floyd really likes to flirt. It bothered me, however, I dismissed it because I didn't want him to think I was the jealous type. Besides, I think jealous types are damaged goods, forever insecure. I'm not the type to be checking up on a man's every move—his cell phone, his roaming eyes, and his whereabouts—I am not any of that."

"Sounds like a sermon I need to preach," I remarked.

Laughing Gianna said, "sho you right."

"Well," Gianna continued, "Floyd's flirtatious ways invited comparisons. 'Why don't you get those extensions like her? Why don't you wear those stilettos? Those are hot!' I was saying to myself, 'I'm not fine enough for you?' But I was stupid enough to fall for it. Told myself I was a progressive sista. So, yes, I painted my nails green with the yellow trim, for him. I wore the brownish, golden extensions, for him. He thought it was sexy like Beyoncé. I just wanted him to know that I was not afraid to be his fantasy. Besides, I just think a woman needs to be flexible with her man. Tastes change, competition is tough, everybody's fashionable; either upgrade or find yourself outdated and without a man! Therefore, I adapted—*for him*."

I noticed how the 'for him' emphasis had a rhythm like a beat, which told me this was not incidental. I wondered to myself, 'How long had she been adapting *for him?*'

"I have watched many sisters lose their man because they couldn't keep...,"

Interrupting, I said, "...Forgive me for cutting you off, Gianna, but you sound like a cell phone—upgradable or replaceable! Cell phones can do amazing things, but they don't have thoughts, they don't have feelings; they surely don't have a soul. Cell phones are dependent on someone else to function. Adapting for him means you were dependent on him; not an equal partner. Healthy relationships involve equal partners."

"Besides," I continued, "fantasies are like a morning mist; here in the morning, gone by noon. If you were nothing more than a cell phone, you only were delaying the inevitable—upgradable, and eventually replaceable! God never called you to be a man's fantasy; you are designed to be a companion."

"Pastor, this is not the first century," Gianna shot back. "That's not how my world turns. Too many women and too few men is my reality—all that puts a lot of pressure on a sista. How can I expect to stay ahead of the game?"

"Get out of the game!" I blurted back as Gianna's eyes widened.

"That's how you stay ahead of the game," I said. "If love is a game, you will always lose. You said it yourself—'you feel like the star in the same old sad movie.' Rearranging the scene and casts never changes the script. The final scene teaches the same lesson—a man will never love and respect you if you are simply his fantasy. In time, even he wants something real!"

Gianna gave a heavy exhale. She heard me, but was not buying.

"Gianna, your point has merit," I said in a conciliatory pastoral tone. "Don't get me wrong. Your times are different and are evolving exponentially. But you need to push the pause button and rethink your strategy. Clearly, it didn't work in this case, did it?"

Gianna's tacit agreement was unmistakable. She knew I was speaking truth. She was stern, however, I didn't want to strangle her sternness. Too often, black women are unfairly attacked and maligned as angry and bitter. Too many black women have had no strong male figures to protect or speak up for them. Thus, they have had to protect themselves. I just want Gianna to be stubborn about Gianna and not just some dude. Many times, black women can be far more stubborn about their men, children, and their careers, at the expense of themselves.

"Think about this for just a moment," as I continued to make my case. "Remember the story of how Laban did the bait and switch on Jacob? Switching Rachel for Leah on the honeymoon night, while forcing Jacob to work seven additional years for Rachel?"[2]

"About the craziest thing I have ever heard, Pastor," Gianna replied.

"It is," I concurred. "We often focus on Laban's treachery. It was so low. We even comment on Jacob's blindness. He never saw it coming. Even in this, can you imagine

---

2 Genesis 29:15-28.

Rachel's anger? To be switched for her sister on her wedding night?"

"It would have been on, Pastor," Gianna working the neck to add emphasis.

"But have you thought about Leah?" I asked.

"No."

"Isn't it interesting that Leah said nothing? Not one word! Leah knew Jacob didn't want her. Yet, she slept with him anyway. She knew full well that Jacob thought she was Rachel, yet she made love to him. You know what that says?"

Gianna just stared at me, not feeling any of it.

"It says Leah was willing to do anything to have Jacob. She was even willing to sleep with him, be his fantasy, be his Rachel, knowing full well, Jacob wanted Rachel, not her. Leah was Jacob's fantasy. Look where that got her," I said.

Gianna exhaled deeply, clearly expressing her frustration with the truth. The truth is difficult. Thank God that Jesus is full of grace and truth.[3]

"Can I ask you another question?"

"I don't know. I didn't care for the last one," Gianna said.

"Cool. I know I can push. You want to call it a day? We can try again later?" I said, as I sensed the tension.

"Naw. I am good. Let's do this. Ask your question?"

"Okay," I said. "Before Floyd, or any other man in your life for that matter, who told you that you were beautiful? No agenda, no game, just beautiful? They are not trying to

---

3 John 1:14.

get with you or hit on you or make you their fantasy. They just admired and affirmed you."

Gianna sat for a moment, thinking. Then a blank stare fell over her face like an evening fog—slow but intruding. She shifted in her seat with a heavy sigh, as if pondering deeper about the question. Still staring, but a bit more serious, now. It was as if she was just informed that her best friend was diagnosed with stage two cancer. Stunned, dumbfounded, and speechless from the bombshell news, not sure what to say. Was she fighting back tears? I was not sure. Finally, she opened her mouth, but nothing came out. A soft, "hmm" finally fought its way out. Then she closed her mouth, still staring, but speechless.

I kept my hand under my chin, index finger over my top lip, ensuring that I remained silent. The counselor's temptation is to interject, to save the counselee; to let her off the hook and return to this feeling at a later time. The truly saving grace, however, calls for the silence; to feel the moment, and grapple with the feelings stirred by the question. Did she need sympathy or did she need challenge? The latter I chose. Besides, Gianna was stubborn. She was no 'punk.' I knew this was a God-moment. Silence is still golden.[4]

Before the ministry, I was an exceptional salesperson; made a lot of money. My strategy? Silence. Ask for the sale and then simply sit, silently. Not a word; no fidgeting,

---

4 Habakkuk 2:20.

not a sound. Like a lion waiting for its prey to make that one fatal move, I waited for buyers to bite. Many bit and bought, reluctantly. Silence does that to you; it makes you say what you wish you hadn't. Buyers, like most people, struggle with the word "no." 'Remain silent' was my motto. Make them say no and explain how your product would not benefit their bottom-line.

Now, the skilled buyer was another matter. It was never personal. They too were lions, marking their territory to let you know, 'I know this game too; but I am the King of this jungle.' I loved it all! I once sat in silence with a buyer for over 10 minutes. The only sound in the room was the ventilation system and an old ticking wall clock. He starred at me like we were playing chicken! I would be lying if I told you I didn't look off. He was a tough hombre. He finally cracked a smile and gave in. It was his way of saying, 'You are pretty tough.' He still purchased what he wanted, but not what I recommended. Well, Gianna was also on the hook.

At last, sitting up with another heavy sigh, Gianna said, "That's a good question, Pastor. My father was hardly in my life. His absence used to bother me; but I just learned to accept it. I was not going to let his absence define my existence."

"Now you can tweet that!" I said.

"Besides Pastor, he's a loser," Gianna continued, "I have no hate for him. I have forgiven him, but that doesn't mean I have to lie about my feelings about him."

27

I knew there was more to the story.

I thought she was ready to answer my question. Instead, another long pause, more staring; thinking, wondering. Suddenly, like dark clouds barreling in on a city, sadness crept in the office. I could feel the momentum picking up. Suddenly, Gianna lowered her head, and while trying to fight back the tears, she softly began to sob.

"Gianna, did I say something to upset you?" I asked. I guess now was the time to let her off the hook. We pastors are not perfect.

"No, Pastor," Gianna said sniffling. "We're good." Gianna grabbed a tissue and wiped a few of the tears that trickled down her face.

"That question caught me off guard," Gianna said, now gathering her strength to respond. "I can't recall one time my father said, 'You are so beautiful.' Not one time. Never had time for me. Always making promises. Never there when I needed him..."

The absence of the personal pronouns referencing her father were strikingly noticeable. I have been pastoring long enough to know that certain ellipses in our language signify a deeper feeling. The unconscious absence of pronouns regarding her father was like the soul's subconscious way of saying, "You were never here; therefore, I will speak as if you are absent." I have witnessed it many times. Her soul was talking now.

"At my high school graduation," Gianna continued, "the one event he did attend, I had on the baaaadddddest dress.

Guys were turning heads. My home girls were gawking big time. My mom was so proud of me. Even Big Mama had to give it up. She loves to cut me up about my clothes. Everyone gave me props on my looks. Him? 'Congratulations Gianna,' is all he said."

Gianna shook her head violently, like the back and forth in a hotly contested tennis match.

"Didn't even hug me," Gianna continued. "Never told me I looked good. Didn't even give me a graduation gift. Before I knew it, poof, gone. Another disappearing act. Didn't even stay for the graduation dinner. I didn't think much of it. Thought maybe he was running from old memories, by seeing Mom and family. I just accepted it; that's his script. It never changes. Runs when it gets good. I never thought about this before, though. He has never told me that I was beautiful." Gianna's last statement was spoken like a detective, after gathering the last piece of evidence at a crime scene.

"Gianna, that affects you," I commented. "The fact that you cannot recall your father's compliment on your beauty? Or even a relative or friend? That affects you."

"Something else got me thinking too, Pastor," as Gianna continued her story. "My mother's brother was always complimenting me on my looks—if that's what you want to call it. I can still hear him now as if I was eight years old; 'Girl, you are going to be something *fine*—umh, umh ummh,'" Gianna said, mimicking the tone and mannerisms of her uncle. Her mimicking had a chill—like how my son, at a very young age, mimicked monsters in his bedroom, in the middle of the night. Frightening.

"That vibe never felt right," Gianna continued. "Shouldn't be saying anything like that to an eight year old girl. Then when I was twelve, he hugged me too close. I knew something was wrong with that at twelve! It confused me. I thought maybe I had led him on. Then later..."

Tears reappeared on Gianna's face.

"...Then later, he grabbed my behind and smiled at me, like he was down. I still cringe. My mother taught me early on, 'under no circumstances, a man has no right to touch your body, unless you give him the green light,'" Gianna firmly stated.

I noticed that Gianna quoted her mother verbatim, with a little acting for good measure. What she may not have realized was that she said it almost with the tone of that little twelve year old. This may be the first time the 12 year old in Gianna had been given a voice.

Gianna continued. "I glared back at him as if to say, 'Leave me the hell alone, you pervert!' I wanted to say it, but didn't. It just wouldn't come out. My eyes did, though. Taught to respect my elders at all times. Sorry, Pastor."

"No issue. He sure made you feel like hell," I quickly said.

"Anyway, it must have scared him because he never attempted that again," Gianna said. "He stayed away from me and I stayed away from him. I never told my mother because I knew it would have devastated her. But sometimes, I think even she doesn't trust him. She rarely invites him over, anymore."

"She may have picked up on it, Gianna, but did not have the ironclad proof to accuse her brother," I pointed out. "Or, maybe she did confront him, privately, banned him from your home, but never told you. Mothers have that eight sense about them. I know your mom, if she had the proof, he would be six feet under and I would have had another funeral under my belt."

Gianna chuckled and said, "for sho. Mom doesn't play that."

"I say that because a lot of mothers don't say anything, even when they know," I said.

"Gianna, God gave you your body," I explained. "It is your body, a gift to you. Under no circumstances does anyone have the right to misuse your body for their personal pleasure. That twelve year old girl was a courageous young lady and ahead of her time. She is still courageous.

"Technically, that was abuse. Please understand this," I said. "That event,—the touching and flirting by your Uncle— is a form of sexual abuse. I know it seems small and incidental, but studies show that such activities affect women emotionally and relationally."

"Man, I didn't know that," Gianna said.

"Yes. Most women dismiss it. But it affects them," I continued. "Gianna, here is your challenge. You have never had a man compliment, value, appreciate, or even celebrate your beauty without an ulterior or sexual agenda. Every man you have encountered has had either no interest in you as a person or solely a sexual interest in your body. That is, they only want you for "what you have;" not for "who you are." They may love your looks, smiles, or the physical features, but they have never valued your heart, your character, your soul, or your personality that makes you, you. Fulfilling relationships thrive with two people, cherishing and protecting the "who you are-ness" in each other. The "what you have" to offer traits, such as looks and physical beauty, are simply the benefits that come with your best you."

"And I'm here to tell you as God's representative without any agenda. You are more beautiful in God's sight than you will ever know. You are God's daughter with a default setting of beauty. Do you believe this?" I asked.

Gianna sat smiling without an answer.

Beauty is skin deep and so much more

"Well, maybe we can talk about that further in a future session. Let's, however, finish our session with some learning," I said.

"I got my notepad, Pastor."

"Cool," I said. "Let's get this thing rolling. Rachel was a woman of astounding physical beauty in her own right. When the bible says, Rachel was beautiful, trust me, she was drop dead gorgeous."[5]

---

5 Genesis 29:17.

"All right now Pastor," Gianna said, smiling.

"You are so funny," I said as I continued. "Beauty, however, was not simply a physical feature in the ancient world. Unfortunately, the modern world limits beauty to body and physical features. This preoccupation with the physical may be why there are so many shattered hearts—focusing on the external at the expense of inner beauty. Granted, physical beauty is wonderful and celebrated by God, but limiting it to the exterior is shallow and fleeting. Rachel had multiple layers to her beauty. As a matter of fact, the Hebrew word for beauty has the idea of a beauty that is breathtaking, attractive, mesmerizing, delightful; but in every possible way—physically, intellectually, and emotionally.[6] Rachel had the entire package."

"Now, I like that Pastor. The total package of beauty!" Gianna said it with great confidence.

"Well, now you can pass it on and help those coming behind you," I advised. "Start a legacy with you! So, today, I want to share with you what your father should have told you about your beauty. I want to suggest to you that there are five layers of beauty to every woman.

~ ~ ~

---

6 Francis Brown, Samuel Rolles Driver, and Charles Augustus Briggs, *Enhanced Brown-Driver-Briggs Hebrew and English Lexicon* (Oxford: Clarendon Press, 1977), 421.

Attractive. "Here I want to start with Leah and redeem her reputation. Historically, the Christian community has been unapologetically too hard on Leah regarding her appearance,

> "Now Laban had two daughters. The name of the older was Leah, and the name of the younger was Rachel. Leah's <u>eyes were weak,</u> but Rachel was beautiful in form and appearance." (Genesis 29:16-17, ESV, Underline mine)

"Weak eyes?" Gianna said, while giving me that crazy look.

"Yeah. It is going to make sense," I assured her. "The manner in which the text juxtaposes Rachel to Leah has led some to deduce that Leah's appearance was "hard on the eyes." The phrases "Eyes were weak" or "weak eyes" has commonly been interpreted to indicate that Leah carried some physical defect, indicative of unattractiveness.[7] That is, she simply may have not been attractive.

To the converse, an alternative view indicates that the word "weak" also can mean "soft" or "delicate." The *Net Translation* of the Bible translates the phrase with "tender eyes."[8] We know that women in the ancient near east wore veils, as many still do today. The only visible feature of a woman were her eyes. So, the standard for beauty in the

---

7 "Eyes were weak" is translated by English Standard Version. "Weak eyes" is translated by the New International Version.
8 Genesis 29:17, Net Bible Translation

ancient world were eyes. Leah had "tender" eyes, or better, different eyes than the standard eyes for beauty.

In this sense, I believe Leah was as beautiful as Rachel. She simply was not Jacob's *type* of beauty. This is a word for all women; *Just because a man is not attracted to you, does not mean you are unattractive*. You are beautiful; you are just not his type of beauty.

"Hmm. Pastor. I like that," Gianna mused out loud. "Everybody has a flavor of beauty and just because your flavor is not the flavor of the month does not mean your flavor doesn't have flow."

"I *think* you got the point," I said, wondering to myself what Gianna just said.

"Yeah. I am Sprite. But if he likes Root Beer, that doesn't mean Sprite doesn't have a good flavor!" Clearly, Gianna was feeling this.

"I think you really got the point," I said. I have to admit— I love the creativity.

"So, Gianna, my word to you is this: What your father should have told you is that you have your own flavor. Just because a man is uninterested in you, doesn't mean you are not beautiful. You are beautiful in your own right. You are simply not his flavor. Therefore, you never have to alter your flavor. Whether a man is interested or disinterested, you are beautiful."

"Thank you *Papa* Pastor!"

"A father serves," I continued, while shaking my head, "to help a daughter embrace her unique beauty. He knows she won't appeal to every man—and she is not meant to. He must assure her that she has her own unique beauty. She does not have to alter her looks or adjust her features to attract a man. Surely, she is free to look her best. No harm in that. Make sure, however that your beauty is a reflection of you and not him. The bottom line is this: No man determines the standard of your beauty! Do it for yourself. Does that make sense?"

"Very much so Pastor," Gianna said.

Composure. I continued with the lesson. "Genesis 29:12 is worth saying out loud, '...and she ran and told her father.'[9] Rachel was a woman of composure. In the moment of stirring feelings of romance, she learned to remain calm, cool, and self-assured. She had composure. This is beauty! For example, even after she discovers her dad's trickery by substituting her for her sister, Leah, on her wedding day, how does Rachel respond? Composure. She remained calm.[10] What bride wouldn't be ticked? On her wedding day? Are you kidding me?"

"I know that's right," Gianna interjected. "Sounds like something my daddy would have done."

"Ease up on your pops now," I said. "Not one time," I continued, "does she go off on her dad, though she has every right to do so. Surely, she didn't agree with the switch.

---

9 Genesis 29:12c.
10 Genesis 29:21-30.

She knows, however, the wise response in the moment is calm and composure."

"Gianna, for the record," I explained, "a woman of composure is a work of beauty for most men. Men love women with composure. Emotional responsibility is incredibly alluring to men. Possibly the most alluring trait of a woman for a man is a woman's prudence and composure. That is, he longs for a woman who ponders and thinks deeply about events, without drawing illogical or ill-informed conclusions."

"That is so hard when you are mad in the moment, Pastor," Gianna replied.

"It is," I concurred. "A woman, however, learns how to modulate the volume of her emotions, while maintaining equilibrium in her disposition. She responds with her convictions and wise rationale and not irrational emotional outbursts. It does not mean she remains silent and simply takes it! It means, she is measured, calm, and remains anchored in her identity. Composure is a dying trait in our culture."

Confidence. "Thirdly," I continued, "Rachel was also a woman of confidence. She could stand on her own two feet. Though she surely wanted to be married, she never exhibited the traits of a neediness for marriage.

> "While he was still speaking with them, Rachel came with her father's sheep, for she was a shepherdess."
> (Genesis 29:9, ESV)

Earlier, we noted that Rachel's shepherding skills indicated a purpose in life. Her skills also indicated self-sufficiency. That is, if by chance she never married, she was secure enough to provide for herself. She needed no man; she had her own money. Her father prepared her to live life on her own, if necessary.

Moreover, her work as a shepherdess further indicated her confidence among men. Though working in a 'male-dominated industry,' she trusted her skill and work ethic to compete. It is interesting to note that Rachel means "ewe," which invariably became her trade of shepherding sheep. Leah means "cow," which also could indicate Leah's trade of working with the family cows.[11] The point I want to make here is that both Rachel and Leah were raised to be self-sufficient. When Rachel met Jacob, she was her own person. If she chose to enter into a relationship with Jacob, she enters as a contributing partner, not as a personal servant."

"That's right, because I have my own money," Gianna said emphatically.

"I know Gianna. Lord knows you have your own flavor too," I replied.

Kindness. "Rachel's fourth layer of beauty was kindness," I explained. "Now, I am drawing an inference from the text to illustrate this idea. She surely had her own issues, but

---

11 This is the author's speculation. The Scriptures are silent on this point.

she never allowed her issues to move her to treat people with disrespect. Not once in this narrative do we see a bitter attitude in Rachel. She was kind.

"Gianna," I continued, "your kindness is far more attractive to men than you will ever know. Guys really have a hard time with loud and salty sistas."

"But Pastor, some bruthas ask for it," Gianna quickly shot back.

"You know I know," I responded. "Not arguing with you there. Hear me out. You can't allow how someone treats you to define you. Just because someone treats us with criminality does not mean we have to react in the same manner. Hold to your dignity; cling to your true self; respond out of your convictions; they all will carry you a long way. To be fair, most women want to be kind, but brothers have mistaken kindness for weakness."

"I'm not weak."

"Not for one second," I replied.

"I surely ain't no punk," Gianna said, smiling.

"Don't remind me," I said smiling back. Gianna was slowly coming back to life.

"No doubt, your mother raised you to be a strong daughter," I continued. "I am saying, however, rethink how you channel your strength. Be more rational in your discussions. Civility goes a long way. Even sworn enemy nations understand diplomatic relations. There is always a place for diplomacy in conflict. If you know a brother won't change, why waste your time? Step."

"You have a point," Gianna acknowledged. "We sistas will argue until Jesus returns, knowing full well we should step. Yet, we just won't."

"Exactly. Why waste the energy if the issue is beyond repair? Stay if there is reasonable thinking. Do not stay at the expense of yourself," I said.

Wisdom. "Lastly," I said, concluding, "Rachel was wise—she made the wise decision, even when her emotions were telling her something to the contrary.

> "Then Rachel and Leah answered and said to him, "Is there any portion or inheritance left to us in our father's house? Are we not regarded by him as foreigners? For he has sold us, and he has indeed devoured our money. All the wealth that God has taken away from our father belongs to us and to our children. Now then, whatever God has said to you, do."" (Genesis 31:14-16, ESV)

Jacob calls Rachel and Leah together for a family meeting. He believes God is calling him to leave Laban's business because of Laban's deceptive business dealings. This, unfortunately, would mean that Rachel and Leah would have to leave their home. Laban had cheated Jacob 10 times.[12] As grandmamma says, 'first time, shame on you, second time...

---

12 Genesis 31:7

"...shame on me," Gianna, completing my sentence.

"Yes," I concurred. "And Jacob sees the handwriting on the wall. It is time to leave. He knows, however, he needs the support of Rachel and Leah. Both Rachel and Leah are wise enough to say in essence, "We know our father has wronged you. We will go with you." Rachel and her sister Leah were able to set aside emotions and make a wise decision."

"Be wise Gianna," I stated as firmly as possible. "Your mother and grandmother are wise women. As a Pastor, I have learned more wisdom from people, than any educational institution I have attended. Most times, the wise decision is the hard decision. It will go against every fiber in your body. It will create an emotional typhoon in us. At the end of the day, however, we know it is the best decision. It takes tremendous maturity to make the wise decision."

Gianna gathered her things and stood to leave, saying, "you really make me think, Pastor. Thanks. See you next week."

Personal and Group Reflection Questions

1) Do you think women ought to "adapt" to their men and be their "fantasy"? Explain. Do women do this more than they should? Why?

_____

_____

_____

_____

_____

2) Who are the men in your life who celebrate you and your beauty without sexual intent? Do you think this affects how you feel about yourself?

_____

_____

_____

_____

_____

_____

3) Has a man touched you inappropriately or sexually abused you? Explain. Have you sought counseling on this and processed this? How has it affected your relationships?

_____

_____

_____

_____

_____

_____

_____

_____

_____

4) What are your thoughts about Leah's beauty? Is beauty simply an issue of "flavor?" Explain.

_____

_____

_____

_____

_____

_____

_____

_____

_____

5) Of all the traits of beauty listed in this section, which trait caught your attention most? Which trait do you believe you need to work on? How does God want you to come to terms with your physical beauty?

Chapter 3

Yes, you need a father's eye

"A lion never loses sleep
over the opinions of the sheep."

~ Anonymous ~

"So, who advised you about Floyd? How did you know that 'he was the one'?" I asked, as I launched into our third session.

"Well, I talked to a few of my friends," Gianna responded.

"Guy or girlfriends?"

"Just my girls," Gianna answered. "I have one friend from college that is usually spot on. She was as shocked at Floyd's actions as I was. I mean, we just missed it."

"Did you talk to family? Mom, others?" I pressed.

"Did all that," Gianna said. "We had been dating about seven months when he met mom. She liked him immediately, especially his southern charm. I mean he was a gentlemen, respectful—won mom on the spot! Mom feels city men have no manners, values, or even faith."

"Introduce him to any men in your family?" I asked.

"No. Not many I trust. I told you about my uncle. That dude..." Gianna stopping mid-sentence, shaking her head.

"...just mom," Gianna finished.

"Your father?"

Gianna just stared at me. I really didn't want to ask the question out of fear that it would sour the remainder of the session. I had to be sure, though.

"So why didn't you introduce him to me?" I asked. "I saw you almost every Sunday for the last year, and didn't see him with you—or did I miss him?"

"No," Gianna answered, "you didn't miss him. He wasn't with me. I don't know why. In hindsight, I guess I should have. Honestly Pastor, you put the fear of God in people. I'm still surprised that I can talk to you about all this. I mean, you cool and all, but you're still a *Pastor!*"

It amazes me how the reputation of clergy continues to plummet, because of so many scandals, yet the perception of 'sacred' remains unchanged. I'm used to it.

"Perfectly understandable," I said. "Not mad at you at all. We pastors don't have the best track record. Besides, who wants to share their soul privately with their pastor who speaks to all the people every Sunday?"

"Naw, Pastor. You're good," Gianna replied. "I've never heard anything even remotely suggesting a breach of confidentiality with you. Just for some, it is a bit uncomfortable."

"Thanks for the kind words," I said. "So, it sounds to me that, ultimately, you were flying by the seat of your emotions in your decision about Floyd. Is that correct?"

"It wasn't just emotions Pastor," Gianna said defensively. "I made a list—assets and liabilities; good and bad traits; good and bad experiences; and the unchangeable flaws I choose to live with—a rational decision. He definitely had more traits I liked, but I underestimated his flaws—especially his flirtatious flaw."

"Did you pick up on the comparison flaw—the flaw we discussed in our previous session? You do agree that is a flaw?" I stressed.

Gianna, now shifted in her seat. Her facial reaction alerted me that she didn't like the question.

"I just didn't think it was a big deal. Everyone compares. That's my dating world. Everything is always changing. Pastor, I don't know what you all did when 'dinosaurs roamed the earth', but it's no biggie for us," Gianna opined.

"Ouch. Turned my own phrase on me," I said, grimacing.

Chuckling, Gianna said, "just messing with you Pastor. I just didn't think it was a major issue."

"But think with me for a second," I said. "If a man can't love and appreciate you, as crafted by the hand of God, could it possibly mean that he has a vision of someone else when he sees you? Could it be that he's shaping and fashioning you into an image he prefers, instead of accepting you as God's gift? So, instead of accepting you for you, maybe he is comparing you to an old flame. Or maybe he is comparing you to his ideal woman, like Beyoncé or some supermodel. Or, God forbid, maybe inadvertently, he is comparing you to his mom!"

"My point is," I continued, "it is not you he wants; it is a repackaged version of you. You are just parts in the creation of the image he wants. So, he never wanted you, which only amplifies the 'you are not enough' feeling."

Gianna shifted in her chair again. I thought I would lose her at this point, but she seemed to remain connected, or at a minimum, interested.

I pressed further. "Secondly, comparisons can indicate a hidden struggle with sex or pornography."

"Really?" Gianna blurted.

"Yes, really. Porn is always about image at the expense of intimacy and relationship. Today's culture of relation-ships is about "intimacy without intricacies," or "friends with benefits." That is, since intimate relationships require so much hard work and can complicate life, this tech-savvy culture says, 'let's keep it simple and keep it sexual.' Let's be intimate without all the emotional entanglements and attachments of commitment that do more to confuse a good thing."

"Furthermore," I continued, "our sexually-saturated soci-ety creates what I call a 'fantasy in the shadows.' That is, our society births and nurtures sexual fantasies that did not fulfill, but still hard to die. Personally, I am not sure if they ever die. Instead, they follow us into other areas of our lives—relationships, family, and yes the sacred bedroom, long after the wedding. The problem is, these 'fantasies in the shadows' also become 'not enough' experiences. No matter how many times one replays or reproduces the fantasies, they're simply 'never enough.'

Unfortunately, many men are duped into thinking there is an ultimate sexual experience, while women think there is an ultimate love relationship. There isn't for either. It is all lies—a fantasy in the shadows. Consequently, many women find themselves doing the unthinkable, trying to measure up to the fantasy, thinking they are doing it for him, out of a love for him. Or, they create a fantasy that 'flips the script' on the man with a passive-aggressive revenge edge.

At the same time, brothers hunt for the ultimate sexual experience only to become emptier than before, because there isn't an ultimate. None of these satisfy. When the house of cards implodes, both men and women bear the hurt and the unalterable emptiness of the fantasy. Women feel victimized, while men feel cheated at the expense of a fleeting unfulfillable experience."

My point had hit home. I saw it in Gianna's eyes. I have often believed that telling people to not have premarital sex was not enough. Most Christian singles know what the Scriptures teach about sex outside of marriage. However, that's not enough. They, also need to know the truth—that is, they need to know why the Scriptures teach what they teach and understand the consequences. I have learned that my role is to point people to God and allow them to make their own decisions as led by His Spirit. God was speaking and Gianna was listening in a far more loving, non-condemning, non-judgmental way.

"This was the one area we were constantly going back and forth on. I mean, every week, it was something new. 'Try this. Let's try that.' I knew something was up," Gianna confessed.

"I'm convinced that this is why so many women struggle with esteem issues," I added. "When a woman falls for the fantasy game, she not only compromises her own identity, but also amplifies her sense of broken esteem, because she is clinging to a fantasy for survival. There is a distinct difference between a fantasy and a real vision."

"Pastor, I have to admit it. You are on point here," Gianna said.

"You loved him so much," I explained, "that your esteem was no longer wrapped up in God who made you. It was wrapped up in Floyd, who you thought would make you feel good about you. No man will ever make you feel good about you. Only the God who made you, can do that."

Gianna sat silently, taking it all in.

I pressed on. "So you were sleeping with him, right?"

I purposely asked the question to invite her to acknowledge the issue openly. Most do, which should be a word to all pastors about the need for compassion. People want honest answers and wholeness on sexual issues. We have to provide the safe place and methods to address these matters. We cannot beat up people for a lack of knowledge. Furthermore, there is just something mysterious and supernatural about confession. It heals and transforms the soul.[13]

"You know I did, Pastor," Gianna admitted freely. "I can't lie. He said he loved me and that we would always be together. Quite frankly, I felt he proved it to me."

"Gianna, you know God's Word and how I have even quoted Beyoncé's lyric, 'Put a ring on it.' It may be your only safeguard and..."

With a heavy sigh of frustration, Gianna interrupted me, "it is just different for us, Pastor! Your generation just doesn't understand. If you were my age, you would not even say this."

"Maybe so." I said. I felt Gianna had taken a huge step.

"Constantly," Gianna said with equal frustration. "He was always wanting to try something new in the bedroom." Gianna appeared embarrassed as she shared this level of intimacy.

"How did it make you feel?" I asked.

"Less than, like you said," Gianna admitted. "Like he was there for the thrill and not for me."

"Well," I quickly replied, "I don't want you beating yourself up. You have been through enough to pile that on. A man that really loves you will accept you for you. No

---

13 James 5:16

pressures. No games. He will protect your honor and cherish your heart."

"Makes me wonder if there are any out there Pastor," Gianna opined.

This is the part I don't like. There is always a truth that hits me back just as hard—sometimes, harder than I would like. She was on point; and I had no answer. This sexually-charged culture makes good men much harder to find. They are out there. The truth, however, is "intimacy without intricacies" or "friends with benefits" is a strong allure for most men, especially young men in their sexual prime. Moreover, many women complicate this issue by doing anything sexually to have a man, which plays perfectly for the 'liberated' man, but damages the sincerely seeking woman. It is unfair.

"Did you forget my 'three coffees and we will see rule' for all dating?

"No. Just knew deep down you would not have liked him," Gianna said.

"I hear you. This is not an inquisition. Sometimes, the "Floyds" are the best lessons to move us toward what God has for us. Gianna. I think that is probably enough sharing for today. Let's move to our lesson."

Father Know Best

"Ready to learn?" I asked.

"Not really. Just not in the mood today. But since I am here, let's do this," Gianna said.

"This is an important lesson, Gianna," I said. "The Scriptures teach that as Christians, we are to hold marriage in high honor.[14] Your desire to date and fall in love, signifies this value. There is nothing wrong with it and I believe God will bless you with marriage in the right time. A father provide the foundational wisdom about marriage for their daughters."

"My mom gives my brother a hard time about women and marriage. Frankly, she is on point most of the time," Gianna added.

"I believe there is a good reason why a father should give away his daughter on her wedding day. Today, this tradition is much more of a formality with very little meaning. Yet, there is priceless value in a father giving away his daughter on her wedding day, in at least two regards.

"First," I continued, "in giving away his daughter, a father is saying to the future son-in-law, 'I trust you with my daughter. I have watched, examined, and vetted you. I have concluded that you are man enough to care and bear the responsibility of marriage to my daughter. Today, along with my wife and family, we give our hearty approval of

---

14 Hebrews 13:4.

you to marry my daughter. I expect you to love, cherish, provide, and remain loyal to her as her husband.'"

"I like that Pastor," Gianna said, smiling.

"Secondly," I continued, "the father also is saying to his daughter, 'I would never give you to any man. You are too special and precious for just anyone. I am entrusting you to this man because I approve of him. I have personally talked, counseled, and vetted him. Therefore, I trust him to be the loving, loyal, husband for you and your family. I expect you to love, cherish, and respect him as God requires. You are free to love him with your heart.' Can you imagine how relationships would fare if fathers vetted men for their daughters in this manner?"

"Absolutely!" Gianna said, shaking her head in agreement. "That would make my life a whole lot easier."

"The irony," I stated, "is that parents in third world countries, countries we incorrectly would declare uncivilized, vet their children's potential spouses with great success. They look beyond the pomp and circumstance of the wedding to the marriage, to ensure their son or daughter has a loving, safe, and trusting spouse."

What Fathers see and Daughters miss

"Let's go back to our study of Laban, in Genesis," I continued. "Though he was notoriously unscrupulous in his business dealings, Laban may have seen things in Jacob that Rachel would have missed. I'd like to suggest to you the same is true for good fathers. Fathers should see things that daughters may miss. I believe there are four traits in Jacob that fathers should help daughters see for a good relationship."

"I need this because I am not *starring* in this movie ever again," Gianna responded.

~ ~ ~

Composure. "First," I explained, "notice that when Jacob saw Rachel for the first time, he lost all emotional control.

"Then Jacob kissed Rachel and wept aloud."
(Genesis 29:11, ESV)

"It's safe to say," I continued, "that Jacob found his rib! Though this was a moment of emotional exuberance, Jacob typically was a man of composure. Even after Laban cheated him ten times, Jacob never lost his temper. This doesn't mean that a man should simply 'take it.' It does, however, speak to his character. How a man handles his emotions says something about his composure. Men need composure to think clearly for engaging relationships. There are numerous Scriptures that advise us to live with composure.[15] As a matter of fact, a trait of the Spirit-filled life is not anxiety, but emotional composure.[16]

15 Proverbs 15:1, 18, Psalm 46:10, Ecclesiastes 10:4, Ephesians 4:26, James 1:19
16 Galatians 5:22-23

Furthermore, composure and integrity may be the twins that indicate that a man walks with God."

"So, I should expect the same from a man, as I would for myself— composure," Gianna added.

"Exactly," I concurred. "If I were your father, I would want to know, does he have composure? How does he handle his emotions under stressful situations? Does he shut down amidst difficult conversations? Does he admit wrong without qualification? How does he handle injustice? Does he blame others for his faults? Does he vent his anger without accepting responsibility for his actions? Fathers know that men of responsibility manage their emotions by growing through their difficulty to become better men."

"Furthermore," I added, "I would have wanted to know his emotional temperature during his successes. Did he get too big on himself? Did he overplay his hand because of a new opportunity? How does he treat people working in subordinate roles? Just because one door opens, does not mean we don't need composure for future doors. I would have wanted to know if he handled his successes and challenges, similarly. Does he have equilibrium?"

"Good stuff Pastor," Gianna commented.

I continued. "I also would have asked him, how was he dealing with what I call the 'father wound'? I'd ask, how does he handle the hurt or pain that may have occurred from the presence or absence of his father? Many men are tempted to use sex, women or any other issue to heal a father wound. They never do. Only time, wise counsel, personal growth and the presence of the Lord can heal a broken heart.[17]

"Finally," I continued, "I would have asked him about his comparison issues. What is driving his obsession with comparisons? Are you comfortable with you? Are you not fulfilled? What will fulfill you? Do you believe God has a greater plan for your life? Do you struggle with pornography? If so, why the obsession?"

Gianna typed notes feverishly on her iPhone, nodding with approval, as I offered my counsel.

Sacrifice. "Second," I continued, "I would have wanted to know about the sacrifices he has made for you."

"For me?" Gianna asked.

"Yes for you," I replied. "If you can't pinpoint at least five specific significant sacrifices in this relationship, there is a good chance that he doesn't love you."

After a purposeful pause, hoping Gianna would volunteer examples, I pushed. "Did he?"

"Sacrifices?" Gianna asked with surprise.

"Yes. Sacrifices!"

"He took me out to nice places to eat," Gianna finally said. "Then again, they were his favorite places. Bought me flowers twice, but that was early in the relationship. He did give up an NBA finals game to talk seriously about our

---

17 Psalm 34:18, 51:17, 55:22, 147:3, Revelation 21:4

relationship. At the time, I thought it was a sacrifice. I think he did it only because I was ready to step."

"Exactly," I said. "You're so smart. There is a distinct difference in a sacrifice to keep the relationship and a sacrifice because one loves you. Most don't know the difference."

"Bet," Gianna laughingly responded.

"Note Jacob's sacrifice," I indicated.

> "So Jacob served seven years for Rachel, and they seemed to him but a few days because of the love he had for her." (Genesis 29:20, ESV)

"Can we agree that my boy Jacob was in love?" I asked.

"Lord, yes," Gianna said with a smile. "That is just too much love."

"It is," I said, "but it captures the essence of sacrifice. Sacrifice is the Christian verb for love. It is the foundation of our faith; Christ our Lord sacrificed himself for us.[18] As people of faith, we are admonished to love others in this manner. A strong indicator that a man loves God and you is his willingness to sacrifice what he cherishes for you.[19] Quite simply, what did Floyd cherish?"

"Ah man, being the life of the party, the latest fashion, Madden NFL, shall I go on?" Gianna asked.

"Had he ever given up any of these for you?" I asked, knowing full well the question was unnecessary.

---

18 John 3:16, I John 3:16
19 Ephesians 5:25

"I got it Pastor. Let's move on," Gianna said.

"Why did Jesus die for us?" I asked. "We were worth it, even though we often feel unworthy. The love of Christ makes us worthy. Likewise, our challenge is always to believe that we are worth sacrificial love. A father has a responsibility to make sure his daughter knows she deserves it. Otherwise, she will always settle. As fathers, we have the added responsibility to share this love with our daughters, so that they'll expect it when a man says 'I love you.' Words lose meaning without actions. So, if I were your father, I would've lived every day expressing sacrificial love to you. As your Pastor, I expect nothing less of myself, my staff, and the people who serve you in this congregation."

"And we appreciate it," Gianna said softly.

Loyalty. "Third," I explained, "I would've looked for loyalty. After Jacob discovered Laban's treachery, he reluctantly accepts Leah as part of the deal to have Rachel.

> "Jacob did so, and completed her week. Then Laban gave him his daughter Rachel to be his wife." (Genesis 29:28, ESV)

Jacob didn't just get Rachel; he got both Rachel and Leah."

"Okay Pastor, this polygamy thing is crazy. Don't know why sisters settled for that mess. You have to admit, we're not that bad!" Gianna said.

"Yes, you are correct," I agreed. "This concept is hard for today's culture to grasp. Unfortunately, in that ancient world and even in some cultures today, a woman's livelihood would've been most often dependent on her husband. Polygamy was the solution to ensure the economic well-being of all women. Though not expedient in the Western world, it was life or death in the ancient world. Most often, a man's livelihood was the only means of survival for a woman."

"I would not have been down for that, regardless," Gianna said emphatically. "I would have found another way."

"Somehow, I could've seen you telling Jacob, 'She has to go or I am out!'" I said with a smile.

"And if he didn't put her out," Gianna continued, "you know I would've!" Gianna is now speaking with the confidence of a woman recapturing her self-esteem. She was finding her voice again.

"Though polygamy is foreign to us," I explained, "it does highlight a truth about any and all relationships. All relationships come with more than what we bargained for. We may expect one thing, but we always get more in return. It happens to all of us."

"So true," Gianna added.

"This was surely what happened to Jacob," I continued. "All he wanted was Rachel, but he got Rachel and Leah instead. Relationships are never ideal and rarely pristine, but often times come with more than what we expect. Jacob, however, embraced it! That's loyalty. He was loyal to Rachel, regardless of what additional issues or baggage she brought. In other words, Jacob was saying to Rachel, 'if Leah is part of the package, I am okay with it. I love you that much.'"

"As I always say," I explained, "love is always a package deal—what you see and don't see is what you get! There are always going to be flaws and issues that we don't like in others. Surely, there're always non-negotiables, such as integrity issues, abuse, violence, etc. Never settle for these. Loyalty, however, rises when we love in spite of flaws or even through flaws. Perfection in relationships is a fantasy, though many unwittingly think it can be had. I'm convinced this is one of the roots of the growing singles' population—thinking one can find the perfect companion, the consummate soul-mate, the one person that fits and gets them. Be careful and don't overplay this hand. There are no perfect mates. The best you can do is be the right person. Loyalty loves in the face of flaws, imperfections, and faults."

Adaptability. "Lastly," I said, "I would want to know about a man's ability to adapt. Jacob learned to adapt to his family situation."

> "So Jacob went in to Rachel also, and he loved Rachel more than Leah, and served Laban for another seven years." (Genesis 29:30, ESV)

"Pastor, that ancient world... I would not have lasted," Gianna firmly said with arms folded. "How can a man love a woman with another woman in the same house? Crazy!"

"Fireworks, to say the least," I said, trying to reconnect. "Never try this at home, right? Two women, living under the same roof, in love with the same man? And the man loves one more than the other?"

Gianna stared in disbelief.

"Okay. Things were very different back then. But hear me out," I laughed. "I'm trying Pastor," Gianna said, sighing.

"There is a great point here," I continued. "Though the Scriptures don't outright condemn polygamy, the story shows its inherent flaws. God easily could have outlawed polygamy; but He didn't. Instead, He allowed it. Why? Sometimes, learning the hard way is the best teacher. Experience is the best teacher, right?"

"Don't I know it," Gianna replied.

"Exactly," I said. "God allowed polygamy, not as an endorsement, but as a learning experience regarding its flaws and consequences. Polygamy, therefore, became a great teaching opportunity—though it was legal, it may not have been wise. This was surely the case for Jacob, Rachel, and Leah as was the case in many other polygamous arrangements.[20] Experience remains the best teacher."

"That actually makes some sense, Pastor," Gianna agreed.

---

20 Exodus 21:10, I Samuel 1-2, 2 Samuel 5:13, I Chronicles 3:1-9, 14:3. Though there were many polygamous relationships in Scriptures, they caused far more harm than good.

"So, for example," I explained, "the Bible doesn't categorically condemn drinking, but it does condemn drunkenness.[21] Yet, we know that many people should never smell alcohol because of the harm inflicted on themselves and others, right?"

"That's true," Gianna concurred.

"Okay," I said. "So, the overarching takeaway is that polygamy, though unfortunately necessary in the ancient world, is not always feasible. The underlying takeaway is that all relationships require adaptability. This simply means that under even the most ideal conditions, no one gets everything they want. Instead, two people must learn to play the hand dealt to them. They must learn to adapt and work together for a greater outcome.

"As a father," I continued, "I would have wanted to know if Floyd was adaptable? Was he willing to evaluate the relationship and make adjustments that benefited the both of you? Sadly, too many men and women make huge adjustments for each other without any expectations in return. A great relationship is based on mutual adaptation, in which both parties are willing to make adjustments for the good of the relationship."

"That's good stuff Pastor," Gianna said, smiling.

---

21 Proverbs 20:1, Galatians 5:21, Ephesians 5:18, I Timothy 3:8. Jesus was accused of drunkenness, which would indicate at a minimum, that he had a drink, Matthew 11:16-19.

Personal and Group Reflection Questions

1) Is your father involved in your life? If so, how much? If not, why?

_____

_____

_____

_____

_____

_____

_____

2) Do you have a male role model, a father's eye, in your life that can advise you about your relationship choices? Explain.

_____

_____

_____

_____

_____

_____

_____

3) Do you think abstaining from pre-marital sex is realistic or antiquated? If so, explain. Do you think pre-marital sex led to what Gianna experienced? Do you think Gianna adapted too much?

4) Under Father Knows Best, which trait appealed to you about men?

5) In your past relationships, were sacrifices made for you, as described in this chapter? Did you make sacrifices? Was there an equal exchange? Explain.

_____

_____

_____

_____

_____

_____

_____

_____

_____

Chapter 4

Yes, sex is always on his mind

"Drink from your own cistern,
and running water from your own well."
~ (Proverbs 5:15) ~

"How long was it after you met Floyd that you slept with him?" I started in like an ambitious district attorney, determined to prove his case. Though the question rung with judgement, I assure you that this was not my goal. We have enough Christians sullying the name of Jesus with judgementalism. I have learned, however, that some of the most important questions feel like judgment, but ultimately lead to faith and freedom.

Gianna sat silent. Normally, I play the silence game to force the issue. This time, I decided to let her off the hook, because no one is ever comfortable talking to their Pastor about their sex life—single or married. Are you?

"Come on, how long?" I reiterated. "I don't want details. No judgment here. You know how I roll. My aim is to help you understand you. Furthermore, I hope to point out some distinctions between male and female sexuality. You cannot assume that sex is the same for men and women."

"I waited two months," Gianna finally answered. "I told myself that I would do the Steve Harvey 90-day-rule, but I couldn't make it. When it gets steamy, it's just..."

"... no details please," I quickly interrupted. "I don't roll like that. Your business is your business. Take it to God. He still forgives and cleanses us from sin. I can guide you—but trust me, I will always guide you back to Him. He can heal your deepest shame, guilt, and struggle. He is able. You know that right?"

"Yeah." Gianna said with sadness in her eyes. I knew she believed it, but sometimes experience will test your heart. It surely was being tested now. God sometimes takes us to difficult places to prove to us that he will do more than what we think or believe.

"So, why two months?" I asked.

"Pastor, I wish you old folks could live in my world," she shot back.

"Like we didn't have struggles?" I replied, with a serious arch in my eyebrow. "What, you think sex was more tempered in my day? More modest? Really? Listen, Solomon was right, there is nothing new under the sun—nothing![22] The only difference between your day and mine is that we hid it better. Trust me, everybody looking saintly on Sunday morning is not saintly. Many are still creeping..."

"Really, Pastor?" Gianna exclaimed.

"I am just saying," I said. "Didn't mean to be crude; sometimes my humor is..."

"...a little off the chain. No problem Pastor, we know you. Why two months?" Gianna asked, repeating the question with another heavy sigh. "Well, at that time," Gianna said, "Mom and I were really going at it. She wanted me out of the house. In hindsight, she was right, but I just wasn't ready. I didn't understand why she was giving me so much heat about it. I guess coming in late at night unnerved her...."

"Mom don't play that," I interrupted.

"No. Mom don't play," Gianna acknowledged, a bit reluctantly. "So, it was one of those times where I really needed another perspective on this—like my dad's. Of course, I wasn't going to call him. So, Floyd and I really connected on it. He inspired me to take the risk, and I can happily say, I'm on my own, now!" Gianna exclaimed, raising her fist in approval, like a cheerleader.

"Cool. You handled your business. Not surprised at all," I said.

"Yeah. He helped me get out on my own. But I didn't need to hear it the way mom was trying to give it to me. I needed..."

---

22 Ecclesiastes 1:8

"...a father's perspective," I interrupted.

"I guess," Gianna said. "At the time, I wasn't sure what I was looking for. But Floyd really understood me. He helped me work through those emotions, which got me thinking that maybe Floyd really loved me. Besides, I have never had a guy take that kind of interest in me.

Well, one night, after another dramatic episode with My mother, he told me he loved me. He beat me to it. Just couldn't believe it. That had never happened before. I was always the first to say 'I love you' in my relationships; rarely heard it in return. It felt good. It felt real good! He said he would always be with me, no matter what. And I believed him. So, I said to myself, 'we're going to be together anyway. What could be so sinful about this?' So, I slept with him."

"Were you sure that was love?" I asked.

"Yeah," Gianna responded with confidence.

"Really?" I asked.

"Well, I know I would learn later, he didn't mean it. But at the time, I can confidently say, Floyd loved me. Why he tripped afterwards, I will never know," Gianna said firmly. She was not going to be moved on her opinion. Though she knew the relationship was over, she was clear about what she felt. It was love.

"Let me educate you about men, like a father should," I said.

"Please!"

"First, for men," I explained, "there is a thin line between love and lust. Pastor A.R. Bernard said it best, 'Love seeks

70

to satisfy others at the expense of self. Lust seeks to satisfy self at the expense of others.' Love and lust look like identical twins but trust me, they have different parents. The only way to distinguish between the two is time. Is he still with you? No. He has moved on, which means, his words to you may have sounded like love. He may have even believed he loved you. If he loved you, however, he would still be with you."

I continued. "Time is always love's best friend. This doesn't mean Floyd is a bad person. It does reveal a deep truth about many men—sex is everything. That is, men are wired to do almost anything for sex. Most women know this in their gut, but refuse to believe it in their heads and hearts. They know men will say and do anything to have it. Time, however, is the best safety indicator to determine if a man truly loves you."

"Not sure I feel you on that one Pastor, but I'm still listening," Gianna replied.

"I don't expect you to understand it because most women don't. But men do not need to be in love to have sex. This is a hard truth for women to accept," I replied.

"Okay," Gianna said.

"Second," as I continued, "Men never fall in love, not at the beginning of a relationship. Men fall in trust."

"Trust? That doesn't make sense Pastor," Gianna now looking at me with the 'brutha you trippin' look that can only come from a sister.

71

"A man," I shared, "falls in trust before he falls in love. If a man trusts you, he will commit to you. Women, on the other hand, naturally connect the feeling of love with commitment. Unfortunately, men do not process love the same way as women. Men can sincerely say 'I love you' and really mean it. But 'I love you' doesn't mean he's ready to commit to you. He commits when he feels he can trust you. Show me a woman a man trusts and I will show you a man whose nostrils are wide open."

"That's old Pastor," Gianna laughingly remarked.

"You got my point, though," I retorted.

"Interesting. Not sure if I agree yet," Gianna stated.

"Question, did Floyd trust you?" I asked.

"Well, he often said he loved me, but now you got me thinking," Gianna replied. "Not sure that he really ever trusted me. For example, when I met his family, he introduced me as his 'girl.' He bragged to his family about me; prepared my dinner plate in front of his his mother, and everything. No man had ever done that for me. But then when I met his friends, he only introduced me as 'Gianna,' almost as if we were buds; like I was one of the boys or something. It didn't feel right."

"Hmm." I responded. "Did you ask him about it?"

"Pastor, you know I did," Gianna said.

"What did he say?"

"'Ah, baby, you know you my girl,'" Gianna said, mimicking Floyd's voice. "Don't sweat me around my boys.

You know you're the one,' he said, buttering me all up. Of course, I bought it and left it at that."

"Here is what you should have said—Nothing."

"Nothing? Pastor, I am not about to be played," Gianna shot back.

"No, you should have said nothing," I said firmly. "You should not have asked him a thing! How he treated you around the boys was his way of telling you exactly how much he trusted you. Your reaction should have simply matched his level of trust. You should have stepped back emotionally, without a word. Nothing."

"Floyd would have gone ballistic!" Gianna blurted.

"So?"

"He would have said, 'There you go again, tripping,'" Gianna mocked.

"Okay. But was he tripping?" I asked.

Gianna just rolled her eyes.

"Gianna," I explained, "you have to see it all as a test. A man does things to test a woman—to see if he can trust her. Bringing you around his boys and treating you like a friend was a test. If you get all bent out of shape about it, that tells him that you're stuck on him, which means he doesn't have to commit to you. It says you'll stick around no matter what. You may get mad, but you're not going anywhere. You will eventually cool off.

If you had matched his trust level, instead, by giving him his emotional distance? You would have forced the issue. He surely forced the issue by treating you like a friend around his boys. Saying nothing and treating him like a friend forces him to think: 'Hmm, she's different. She didn't fall for that. I can't play her like the others. She is her own woman. I like that.'

See, deep down inside, men fall for women who will stand up for themselves. Now, that doesn't mean he wants you in his face with the sista attitude, which many women mistake. It just means, he recognizes that you respect yourself enough to not be walked over. If he can play you, he'll never commit to you. You can bet on that like the resurrection. Many sisters really misunderstand this. It is true that some guys are heartless; others are immature. Some, however, are testing the waters. They want to know, 'Are the waters pure or polluted? Can I trust you?'"

"Interesting Pastor," Gianna replied.

"Of course, this is something your father should have told you," I remarked.

"Of course!" Gianna replied with a smile.

"Most sisters are unaware of it," I continued. "I know it feels like games, but it is just the way men socialize. Men don't depend on emotions to test people; they trust their instincts. They watch you like a leopard on an antelope. I call it the *predatory instinct*. All men have it. Trust me on this one. When men come to church, they are watching me like a hungry leopard! One wrong word or move, they are out! Who knows? I might get a nasty Facebook post. All men have it, the predatory instinct. Likewise, if he is testing you, that fact alone indicates his high level of interest in you. He is just not sure if he wants to lay it all on the line for you."

"Now unfortunately," I further explained, "some men are destructively predatorial. They didn't have the father or father figure to train or model the proper use of their predatory instinct. Thus, many men are on a quest, searching for their manhood through trial, error, and ultimately conquest. He measures his manhood by the success of his predatory instinct. Unless he is taught or trained, he remains a menacing predator, doing far more damage to himself and those close to him.

"Sadly," I continued, "most men are unaware of how this affects them. On the one hand, they really don't know what to do with it, knowing that underneath the skin, there is something far greater wanting to be unleashed. Imagine if he channeled all that energy into a worthy cause, like fighting injustice? On the other hand, giving in to it leaves him empty, lonely, and depressed, which may ultimately sabotage him. Therefore, many men never live out an authentic manhood of leadership, maturity, and life-purpose. He is a life-giver in more ways than he can ever imagine."

"I thought sistas had issues! Not like yawl!" Gianna commented.

I could only laugh, saying, "Flesh and blood did not reveal that to you." My mentor loves to use that phrase.

I continued. "Now, you missed that test—a test among friends. But the ultimate test was the sex test. He may have been there for you, but trust me, he was testing you. Remember this for as long as you live; even if a man loves you with all his heart, the sex is always a test. Always. You can rest your hat on that one," I said.

"A test, huh?" Gianna wondered.

"It is either a test or a meal, to feed the appetite, tells you nothing about love," I remarked.

"Men have issues." Gianna blurted again in frustration.

"You have no idea the pressures of sex on a man. That's why it takes a mature man to handle his sexuality in a loving responsible way," I concluded.

Seven years is worth it!

Gianna may not have agreed with my assessment of her relationship with Floyd, but she was eager to learn. I only had hoped to provoke her thinking. I have to trust God to do the rest. Is there a better way?

Gianna proudly whipped out her iPad to take notes and said, "let's do this."

"Okay then. Let's finish this session," I concurred. "If you want a good picture of a man's sexuality, Jacob is a great example. I want to give you four simple reminders about male sexuality. Write this text down.

"So Jacob served seven years for Rachel, and they seemed to him but a few days because of the love he had for her. Then Jacob said to

Laban, "Give me my wife that I may go in to her, for my time is completed."' (Genesis 29:20-21, ESV)

"First, *A man's true love rises above sex*," I stated. "Jacob waited for Rachel for *seven years!* Did you get that?"

"Yeah. He kind of punked out for her, didn't he?" Gianna remarked.

Laughing, I said, "from our vantage point, maybe. But it does bring home an important trait about mature male love. Jacob was willing to sacrifice seven years of his life for her. True love always rises above sex. And I'm going to ask you a question: 'Are you worth seven years?'"

"Pastor, I'm not going to lie. I'm not waiting seven years!" Gianna said, unapologetically.

"That isn't what I asked you," I quickly shot back. "Are you worth seven years? Gianna, it's not about what you're *feeling*; it's about what you *value*. Do you value yourself enough to know you are worth seven years?"

"That is a good one Pastor," Gianna said.

"As I said earlier, time is your greatest ally. A man who loves you, values you enough to wait for you," I said. Of course, I noticed that Gianna never answered my question.

"The second thing," I said, continuing, "notice what Jacob said to Laban, Rachel's father: 'Give me my wife that I may go into her...'[23] I always laugh at a text like this because the ancient Biblical culture was far more direct about sex

---

23 Genesis 29:21b.

than today's church culture. Jacob knows that the wedding night is upon him. He's upfront about it, too. *'Give me my wife that I may go into her...'* In other words, 'I want to have sex with Rachel, now!' Try telling a daughter's father that today."

"And I thought I was straight to the point," Gianna replied.

"This is a hard one for women," I explained. "Romance, affection, and trust are important; but when it comes to marriage and love, *sex is love for a man*. Granted, men can become addicted to sex like anything else. But a man does not commit to one person to be a monk. He wants sex and he wants it often. It sometimes may not feel like love to you, but it is love to him." *Sex is still everything for men, even after love!*

"I just don't see that as being a problem before or after marriage," Gianna said.

"Well," I replied, "it usually isn't before marriage; but after marriage? It often becomes a huge issue. As a single, however, you have to be careful not to allow sex to dominate the relationship. If sex is everything before marriage, love will almost be nothing after marriage."

"Third, *for men, sex can purely be physical, even after love*," I stated.

"What?" Gianna said with shock.

"You heard me right," I said. "Physical. Women tend to see sex in emotional and relational terms. Men can connect with sex in those ways as well, but they also can have sex in a purely physical sense, without any feelings of love. This is hard for women to imagine, since women see the world through the lens of relationship. Men, on the other hand, can turn their emotions on or off, even with sex."

"Cra, Cra, Crazy! That doesn't make any sense Pastor," Gianna exclaimed.

"I know," I said. "That is because men are nothing like you. When you get home, I want you to read Genesis 30:1-4. To summarize, Jacob has two wives—Rachel and Leah. They are both fighting each other to have sex with him. Now remember, Jacob loves Rachel. Worked seven years just to have her, remember?"

"Yes, Pastor," Gianna said.

"But Rachel cannot have children. So what does she do? She offers her female servant to Jacob as a means for having children. Does Jacob love Rachel enough to object? Hardly. He accepts the opportunity for more sex, which Jacob enjoys. Now, he still loves Rachel, but he is a man who loves the physical connection of sex. His love never changed for Rachel, even though he had sex with her servant!"

"I'm not feeling that!" Gianna blurted.

"My point is," I continued, "sex can be purely physical for men. I am not condoning the behavior, but men experience sex differently than women. Don't forget that. You may be thinking one thing; he surely can be thinking another."

"Lastly," I said, concluding, "*sex will never make a man love you.*"

"I think I know that, Pastor," Gianna said firmly.

"Cool, then here is something to pass on to your running partners," I responded, knowing that Gianna would continue to take in the information for herself. Genesis 29 says the following:

> "Again she conceived and bore a son, and said, "Now this time my husband will be attached to me, because I have borne him three sons." Therefore his name was called Levi. And she conceived again and bore a son, and said, "This time I will praise the LORD." Therefore she called his name Judah. Then she ceased bearing." (Genesis 29:34–35, ESV)

I said, "This is the story of Leah's attempt to get Jacob to love her. How did she do it? Sex. She thought that if she gave him sex, Jacob would love her. The bad news is that Jacob never loved her. This is a hard truth for women to accept. You can sexualize the relationship as much as you want—that will not guarantee love or devotion from a man. If it is true that men give love to get sex, then it is equally true that women give sex to get love."

"Can't argue with that," Gianna commented.

"The only drawback is that it never works. Men have to choose to love a woman. The good news for Leah is that, this painful experience drove her to the Lord.[24] God can

---

24 Genesis 29:35.

use our bad decisions to bring about a good end. The Lord is extremely merciful to us, if we would just trust him."

"It is refreshing to know that the Lord loves us like that," Gianna said, smiling.

.

Personal and Group Reflection Questions

1) Do you believe Gianna sexualized her relationship too quickly? Why or why not?

_____

_____

_____

_____

_____

_____

2) Are you sexually active? If so, why or why not? How quickly have you sexualized a relationship? Do you think sexualizing a relationship contributes to the problems in the relationship? Explain.

_____

_____

_____

_____

_____

_____

_____

3) Do you agree or disagree with the Scripture's perspective on premarital sex? (I Corinthians 5:1, 6:18-20, 7:8-9, Hebrews 13:4). Is premarital sex a sin? Is abstaining from premarital sex realistic to you? Does premarital sex damage relationships, long term?

4) Do you believe men and women view sex differently? Is this important to know in building a healthy, flourishing relationship?

5) Did you learn anything about male sexuality that surprised you?

_____

_____

_____

_____

_____

_____

_____

_____

_____

Chapter 5

Yes, you have an issue

"We cannot solve our problems with the same
level of thinking that created them."
~ Albert Einstein ~

"Always great seeing you Gianna," I said, as I welcomed her into my office.

"Always glad to be here, Pastor," Gianna replied with a confident smile—a smile that communicated progress.

Though Gianna was still working through her recent breakup with Floyd, she indeed was showing remarkable signs of charting a new path for herself. I'm not convinced that anyone totally recovers from a painful breakup such as Gianna's. We may learn to live with it or learn to live in spite of it. We may even press through the pain desperately hoping that it will subside with time. Make no mistake, however, the injury remains with us.

There are two realities about our emotional injuries. First, an injury may remain dormant within us, waiting for the opportune moment to reappear. We feel the pain from the initial injury, but like all injuries, with time, the pain subsides. The injury, however, remains with us, and in most cases may never completely heal. Yet, under the "ideal" conditions, the pain of the injury hijacks our actions with alarming surprise. We say to ourselves, "I thought I was over this." In truth, we are over it; the injury, however, remains within us. A wrong memory or a familiar song can trigger it with the surprise of a striking cobra.

Second, if we are not careful, we may integrate the injury into our true selves. Thus, unconscious to us, the injury invariably takes on a persona that influences us. It will shape our actions, attitudes, and even our feelings. This reality is very destructive and can quietly and covertly infect us like a cancer. Unfortunately, by the time we diagnose it, it has done far more damage than we possibly can imagine. The injury has subverted our true identity. We no longer love, laugh, and trust like we should. The injury now has its own personality and emotions, making its voice virtually indistinguishable from our true voice.

The good news is that Gianna has chosen to address her injury instead of ignoring it. It, undoubtedly, will remain with Gianna; but it will not define her. She realizes, like all injuries, it leaves an emotional wound that requires attention and time. By acknowledging and embracing the breakup, however, Gianna learns that the breakup does not have to redefine or subvert her. This is fundamental for understanding how God brings us through our pain, injuries and breakups.

"Gianna, I think you are progressing through this and I have to say, I am very proud of you for staying with the process," I encouraged her. "I am not going to lie to you, I don't think anyone is ever totally free of a painful experience. Instead, we learn from it so that it does not define or control us."

"Thanks Pastor. Just trying to get through it," Gianna replied.

"You are doing it too," I acknowledged. "Today, I want to approach our session differently and launch right into an issue that I believe many women either ignore or do unknowingly."

"Okay Pastor," as Gianna readied herself.

"I want take another look at Leah, the sister of Rachel," I stated. "If you recall, we talked about how Leah is often unfairly labeled as the ugly sister nobody wanted. I take it that she was beautiful, but with her own...

"...flavor," Gianna quickly blurted, completing my thought. "Oh, sorry Pastor. I couldn't resist that one."

"That's okay," I replied. "Tells me that you're learning. I want you to have your own flavor. By flavor, of course, Leah had her own sense of beauty and simply needed to accept it. In time, God would send her someone who cherished her beauty. But also, like most women, Leah struggled with what I call the *helper gene."*

"The what?" Gianna said.

"The helper gene. Hear me out," I continued. "The helper gene is a trait that I believe God put in all women. It rears its head first in Genesis 2:18. Pull it up on your smartphone,

> "Then the Lord God said, "It is not good that the man should be alone; I will make him a <u>helper</u> fit for him."" (Genesis 2:18, ESV, Underline mine)

Now, many misconstrue "helper" to mean that women have been regulated to a coach seat existence in male/female relationships. Instead, the description reveals something deeper about the nature of all women. More to the point, the word is actually a positive word and is used to describe the very character of God.[25] God is a God who helps us, coming to our aid in our time of need. God has a natural inclination, a "knee-jerk" reaction if you will, to help people. It is an irresistible urge lodged within the character of God, if we could say that God has urges.[26] Plainly stated, God cannot help but help people."

---

25 Deuteronomy 33:7, Psalm 27:9, 40:17, 46:1, 118:7, 124:8, 146:5.
26 God is not like man, especially in human frailties as stated in Numbers 23:19. The biblical writers, however, will use what is called "anthropomorphisms," that is, human metaphors to help us understand the character of God. Thus, I am using "urges" as an anthropomorphism to help Gianna capture God's inclination to help.

"God is really good," Gianna added.

"He is," I concurred. "In this sense, Gianna, God made women with this natural inclination to help people, the helper gene.[27] Like God, many women have an irresistible urge to help."

"Sounds like My mother," Gianna said.

"Exactly," I said. "It's like the mothering instinct, in which mothers will give everything possible to their children, even at the expense of themselves. God put it in mothers and women to ensure that a child would never go unloved. Whether it's a mother, grandmother, or a loving aunt, women have the helper gene."

Gianna, nodding as she continued typing notes on her iPhone.

"Now," I further explained, "here is the Achilles heel of the helper gene. What should be reserved for children, family or a noble purpose, women intuitively give to men for *love*. Unfortunately, women believe that by helping men they can secure love for themselves. Thus, instead of allowing the relationship to develop naturally, women will help move the relationship toward love. Leah is a great example of the gene. She thought that if she gave

---

27 It should be noted here that the helper gene, especially in the context of marriage, may create the greatest problems, if not properly understood. Whereas men struggle with a control gene, women can overstep a man's personal boundary by attempting to help him—when he has asked for none. This sincere intention to help can easily be misconstrued as manipulation, control, and subversion, creating greater distance and conflict in a marriage. Wives must exercise care and control in seeking to help their husbands with their sincerest intentions.

her husband Jacob more children, he would love her in return.

> "And Leah conceived and bore a son, and she called his name Reuben, for she said, "Because the LORD has looked upon my affliction; <u>for now my husband will love me</u>."" (Genesis 29:32, ESV, underline mine)

> "Again she conceived and bore a son, and said, "<u>Now this time my husband will be attached to me</u>, because I have borne him three sons." Therefore his name was called Levi." (Genesis 29:34, ESV, underline mine)

Leah gave Jacob children, believing it would help Jacob love her. Unfortunately, it never happened. I will say that again, Gianna, it never happened. As a rule, it rarely happens. And when it does, the woman usually becomes the controlling voice in the relationship, which only deepens the dissatisfaction—always fussing and never satisfied, while dictating the course and activity of love. Love does not operate in that manner. You cannot control love. You cannot make people love you. People love you because they choose to love you."

Gianna now sat noticeably silent. She ignored my pause, as if she was waiting for more information.

"My point here," I continued, "is not to pile guilt on you, Gianna. Instead, know that this tendency is in you. Don't run from it. Don't deny it. Admit it. Acknowledge it. It lives deep in you. It'll hide, play dead, and even disguise itself as Mother Teresa. It'll spiritualize itself and mask the voice of the Spirit, saying, 'You are just doing what Jesus would have done.' Don't fall for it. Own it before it owns you. True love—*loves freely*. Therefore, if Floyd really loved you, he would've loved you because he wanted to love you."

Gianna now stared into blank space as I concluded my thoughts. After five sessions, the meaning of the silence was obvious to both of us. Truth had found its bulls eye; and it was unsettling. Gianna sat very quietly, her infectious smile, now in a half-arched frown. I too, sat knowing that these moments, though emotionally disrupting, can be the breakthrough in the path of recovery.

Breaking my own silence rule, I finally spoke up. "What are you thinking?"

After a deep sigh, Gianna finally said, "I still love him and I don't know what to do with it." Grabbing a Kleenex from the box on my desk, Gianna wiped a few tears that trickled from her left eye.

"Well, I think Floyd always will have a place in your heart, but the feeling, over time, should subside," I replied. "It's a normal process. I think you are still on track, being honest with where you are. Look at it this way, you cannot change your destination overnight, but you can change your direction today. You are changing your direction and that is most important. The destination always takes more time."

"That's good to know. Seems like an awfully long journey through this," Gianna said, still wiping tears away.

"It is," I concurred. "So, you tried to help him love you, didn't you?"

"In hindsight, I guess if that is what you call it," Gianna replied. "I thought I was being the 'mature' woman, by wearing what he liked. Now, I have to admit that I did it to get him to love me. Clearly it didn't work," Gianna, shedding more tears, fighting the sobbing that wanted out.

"It hurts Gianna," I said, as Gianna covered her face with muffled weeping. I waited, while she wept.

"I'm sorry Pastor," Gianna wiping her face, trying to cover up her crying.

This has always baffled me. How did we get to the place where crying is almost criminal? Even for women today, it is viewed as weakness. Many cultures expect tears after difficulty. It is painful. The natural response is tears. Today, however, public displays of grief are shunned. It is dishonorable, a sign of weakness, yet it is the first and healthiest means of recovery. Crying is the body's way of acknowledging the pain. Those who cry experience a higher rate of recovery than those who don't.[28] Yet, we persist with the

---

28 Various articles. "Eight benefits of crying: Why it's good to shed a few tears" by Laura Burgess, accessed at https://www.medicalnewstoday.com/articles/319631.php. "Is Crying Good for you?" by Serusha Govender, accessed at https://www.webmd.com/balance/features/is-crying-good-for-you#1. "The Health Benefits of Tears" accessed at https://www.psychologytoday.com/us/blog/emotional-freedom/201007/the-health-benefits-tears.

'stick to our guns' approach, suppressing our true feelings. Gianna's soul was fighting to release the infection trapped within.

"No issue," I said. " Your heart is doing what comes natural. Take your time."

After a few more sniffles and face wipes, straightening herself up, Gianna said, "I just didn't realize that I still loved him that much."

"Yeah, this won't be the first time it will sneak up on you," I said. "So, in what ways did you try to help him love you?"

"Well, definitely with my dress. Told myself that I was being a 'liberated woman.' I wasn't afraid to travel toward new frontiers. So, I adapted. I also wanted him to know I wasn't the jealous type. I had seen it too many times. I wanted to present myself as a confident and secure woman. But now I realize that I allowed my helping gene to get the best of me," Gianna said. The regret was evident in her tone.

"So, what does that tell you?" I pushed.

"I'm not sure what you mean. I admitted that I tried to help him love me. What is your point?" Gianna asked, defensively.

Now, the hard part of my job is helping people discover the truth for themselves. I am a preacher and by nature, I love speaking God's wisdom to help people experience a better life. Nothing thrills me more than to see people flourish.[29] I have learned, however, that people really change when they discover the truth for themselves, instead of hearing it from me. How many times did we hear the truth from our parents or some respected elder? Countless times. Yet, many of us still walked our own way.

It wasn't until we discovered the truth for ourselves that real change happened. I so desperately want to tell Gianna the truth, like a father would want for his daughter. That is how pastors are about their flock. Yet, the sage in me, instinctively, knew that she needed to learn this herself. God is a teacher. He rarely gives us the answers in advance because, He knows we will not apply what we learn. Personal discovery may be God's favorite teaching tool. It helps us move from despair to wholeness.

"What does this tell you, if you had to help him love you?" I asked.

"Oh," Gianna sighed deeply. "He really never loved me?" Gianna dangling the question as if she was not sure. Maybe, the question was a glimmer of hope that Floyd did love her. But, deep down inside, Gianna knew the answer. The soul often fights the truth.

"You tell me what you think," as I continued to fight the urge to answer the question for her.

Gianna thought for a moment before answering. "I think he wanted to love me. He may have even loved

---

29 Jeremiah 29:11, Matthew 6:33, Luke 6:38, John 10:10, James 1:17.

me, but was still unsure. I don't know Pastor. This is so hard!" Gianna threw up her hands and slumped back in her chair.

"You are doing well. It is work, but work is the way out. So stay with it. There is a valuable lesson here. What does this tell you?" I pushed.

"Maybe he loved me, but not at the level I needed love," Gianna said with more confidence.

Gianna really was starting to underrated the truth about herself. "Okay," I said. "Now, I'm ready to give you my opinion, because you are pressing through."

Gianna attempted to smile through her tears.

"I cannot say categorically that Floyd loved you" I said, "because I didn't know Floyd. But, I think your assessment is correct. I think you are right that he wanted to love you and, may in fact, have loved you. But his love for you was not at a commitment level. It may have been growing, but it had not matured. Or, it could have simply been lust, but personally, I don't think it was just that. But, I will agree that it was not at the level you needed. I think he loved you. But he was not ready to say 'You are the one.' You, however, were ready to say to Floyd, 'You are the one.'

All relationships have levels of love. You have to assess the levels, logically and not emotionally. Ask yourself, 'Am I at a Level 9, when he may be at Level 3'? If you know your love level is greater than his, you must be careful and wise. Why? Because he has to choose to go to the next level of love for you. You cannot choose for him. My point in all this is, you want to learn how to assess love before you give love. Does that make sense?"

Gianna, nodding, as she said, "Yes—something my father should have told me, right?"

"Yes," I said, "something your father should have told you. The truth is men just process love differently from women. If a woman feels love, it is real to her. She will act upon it much quicker than a man will. Men can feel it and never act. Men can fall for women at first sight, but most are not ready to commit. Just remember, women and men process love differently."

Awareness

"Gianna," I said, "it takes great courage to work on our personal issues. We all have them. Most people, unfortunately, ignore them, hoping they will disappear. They never do. You, however, have chosen to work through them so that you can become a stronger person. God will honor that."

I really wanted to encourage Gianna because she has exhibited a keen ability to press through her most searing pain. She is a strong, young woman who is not afraid to challenge difficulty.

"Thank you Pastor," Gianna replied. "I feel like I'm headed in the right direction. Mom taught me that in time, everyone's path leads to a valley. But like David, we have to walk through it; not dwell in it," Gianna sermonized.

"Preach Gianna!" I kidded with a chuckle. "That is wisdom for me. I want wrap up this session with an issue that I think is invaluable for working through difficulties. I think it is especially important for woman with the helper gene."

"That helper gene is in me. I can't deny that. This has been very helpful, Pastor. I am aware now," Gianna added.

"Aware is exactly what I want you to take away today. Have you heard of the term self-awareness"? I asked.

"Yes, I have Pastor. As a nurse at Methodist hospital, I was given extensive training on the subject. The hospital wanted us to be aware of our actions and emotions to offer better care and sensitivity to our patients. It has been an invaluable tool that has helped me carve out greater meaning in my work and greater compassion for my patients. I really feel like I'm helping people instead of punching a clock," Gianna elaborated.

"Well stated, Gianna," I affirmed. "In a word, 'self-awareness' is the ability to know ourselves—that is, our thoughts and emotions, and the actions that drive us to act or do.[30] Self-awareness is the process of understanding why we feel and react the way we do. Many times, knowing what we are doing is a great first step in identifying our inner issues. Knowing *why* further helps us work through them. So think of self-awareness as something like the peeling of an onion, layer by layer. Every time we peel away a layer

---

30 Bradberry, Travis. Emotional Intelligence 2.0 (p. 61). TalentSmart. Kindle Edition.

of our thoughts and emotions, we gain greater insight into who we are and why we do what we do. What I want to teach you today is not simply to avoid another heartbreak, but to understand why you were attracted to Floyd. For example: Why did you fall so hard for Floyd? Why did you miss so many behaviors in him that are now so obvious? What does your love for Floyd say about you and your emotional wiring? Knowing why you feel the way you feel is the process of becoming stronger. This is the path through that dark valley your mother taught you about."

"I don't know why I didn't make the connection of self-awareness, that I learned on my job, with my relationship with Floyd," Gianna explained. "I mean, at the hospital, we're always talking about being aware of our emotional selves when engaging patients. I just never thought of it in my relationship with Floyd."

"That's okay. I'm glad you're familiar with the concept. It should be very easy for you to implement, personally," I assured her.

"The ancient Biblical followers of the faith were keenly aware of themselves, in their walk with God," I continued. "It was a practice that was instrumental to their growth and development as people of faith. There are a number of Scriptures that identify this practice,

"Examine me, O Lord, and try me; Test my mind and my heart." (Psalm 26:2, NASB95)

"Search me, O God, and know my heart; Try me and know my anxious thoughts; And see if there be any hurtful way in me, and lead me in the everlasting way." (Psalm 139:23-24, NASB95)

"Examine yourselves, to see whether you are in the faith. Test yourselves. Or do you not realize this about yourselves, that Jesus Christ is in you?—unless indeed you fail to meet the test!" (2 Corinthians 13:5, ESV)

The last verse is based on the church's time-honored worship practice, the Lord's Supper. As followers of Christ, we are to live a life of self-examination, or self-awareness. The Lord's Supper is a time in which followers of Christ pause and reflect on the state of their souls. On the one hand, it connects us to the living presence of Christ and his promises.[31] We are never alone. Christ is always with us. On the other hand, it helps us to reflect on our soul's condition. We should ask ourselves questions like, 'Where are we really in our walk with God? Are we as close to God as we think? What is really driving our actions and attitudes?' Do you remember what God asked Adam after he had eaten the forbidden fruit?"

"Where are you Adam?" Gianna responded like a biblical scholar.

---

31 Matthew 28:20, John 14:20, Romans 8:38-39, Hebrews 13:5, I John 4:4.

"I knew I had someone in my church that knew their Bible," I quickly applauded. "'Where are you, Adam?' is correct. God did not come condemning Adam for his obvious transgression. Instead, God wanted Adam to become aware of his actions and the consequences. 'I know where you are', God says to Adam, 'but Adam, do you know where you are? Do you know the implications of your actions? Do you know how this one act has affected your soul? Your relationship with Me? With Eve? Your future?' We gravely undervalue the benefit of self-awareness.

"It amazes me how what I may learn on my job is connected to my spiritual life," Gianna said.

"It's all connected," I replied. "So today, I want to give you *four* things to practice that can help you dive deeper into the area of self-awareness."

~ ~ ~

Observe closely your emotional highs and lows. "First," I explained, "try your best to note your emotional mood swings—especially the extremes. It's easy to assume that our emotional highs and lows are routine. To become emotionally aware, we must identify those mood swings that descend upon us. You don't want to overanalyze this. You simply want to note the mood swing. Did you suddenly become sad? Why are you so chipper? Make a note of places, times, events, or conversations that may have ignited your mood swing. Maybe a song triggered a painful memory or a phrase recalled a joyful one. This step will help you begin to observe your emotional wiring."

Learn your emotional buttons. "Second, learn your emotional buttons," I furthered explained. "Trust me, you have them. We all have them. If we don't learn them, they will be the invaders that drive us off the emotional reservation. For me, as you know, the unjust treatment of African-American people drives me to emotional insanity," I said with emphasis.

"Do we ever know, Pastor," Gianna said, shaking her head.

"Would not be called of God, if I weren't angry about something," I said in response. "As a Pastor, I need to remain ever aware of this reality. Otherwise, it may consume me and cause greater harm than good. If I lose my temper about injustices against African-Americans, what makes me think I can't lose my temper with the people I love, such as my wife and sons, or the people God calls me to lead? The Bible offers us very wise words here: "'be angry, but sin not.[32]'"

"I get that," Gianna acknowledged.

"Learn your hot buttons," I continued. "Also, don't assume that your hot buttons are only negative. One time, I was negotiating the price of a car with a rather slick car salesman. We had come to a stalemate in the negotiations and I was about to walk away from the purchase. He

---

32 Ephesians 4:26

pulled a quick sales trick on me, by appealing to my ego, saying, 'Mr. Autry, you are clearly a smart man. You never would have arrived at your place of success without your smarts. I need to acknowledge that and see it more your way.' What did he do? He appealed to my ego to get me back to the bargaining table. I would be lying to you if I said I didn't like it. It almost worked, where, I almost caved to his price offer for the car. It generated a good feeling that could have been a financial mistake. We tend to look for the negative hot buttons, but trust me; your positive ones may be more damaging."

Pause and reflect on your emotions. I continued. "Third, I always encourage people to keep a journal of their emotional moments. What did the emotion make you feel? What did it make you remember? What can you learn about yourself from this moment? About God? What do you need to do in the future to guard against this reaction? Self-reflection is a lost art in our culture. We would experience greater happiness if we took time to pause and reflect on our emotional moments."

Employ awareness practices to grow through your emotional highs and lows. "Lastly," I said, "here is where the work begins. Employ practices for working through those emotional highs and lows. For example, my anger button requires deep pause before I respond. When I am angry, I have to remember that the issue is in my emotional brain.

Thus, a moment of calm allows my anger to subside, which moves the thought from my emotional brain into my rational brain. This approach allows me to think far more clearly about the issue and my feelings. If I respond in the moment, I'm sure to regret the result. If I wait, even count to fifteen, I tend to respond with far more calm and reason. Granted, I'm not going to always be silent about controversial issues. The calm, however, forces me to release it emotionally so I can address it tactically and rationally."

"No doubt," Gianna inserted.

"So," I continued, "over time, I am learning that as the deep pauses and reflections increase, my temper temptations decrease. Now, those temptations are still with me; and sometimes they growl and bark! With self-awareness, however, they are less likely to control me. I still have my moments, but I'm progressing.

'Thank you Pastor. I never leave here without a lot of food for thought. You really push me, " Gianna said.

Personal and Group Reflection Questions

1) Do you agree that women have a tendency to push men to love them? Explain.

_____
_____
_____
_____
_____
_____

2) Do you think relationships should develop naturally? If so, do you think we fight this process?

_____
_____
_____
_____
_____
_____
_____

3) Do you agree with the idea of the "helper gene"? If so, how has it helped or hurt you in your relationships?

_____

_____

_____

_____

_____

_____

_____

4) Are you aware of your emotions? Are you prone to emotional outbursts? Are you perceived as one with "attitude"? Explain.

_____

_____

_____

_____

_____

_____

_____

5) Do you think self-awareness can help you? Do you plan to keep a journal of your emotions?

_____
_____
_____
_____
_____
_____
_____
_____
_____

Chapter 6

Yes, this will hurt you

"Throw me to the wolves and
I will return leading the pack."
~ Anonymous ~

As I prepared for Gianna's sixth session, I felt a compelling need to pray. Like Jesus, who knew the pain that was ahead of Him on the cross, I also knew the pain that was ahead for Gianna. Surely, she was progressing and growing, but this upcoming session was essential. I have learned that if we follow Jesus long enough, we too, will face our own cross. Unfortunately, there are no detours around it. We might freeze, fight or even take flight, but in time, we will discover that the path forward is through the cross. It awaits us all with all its shame, discomfort, and agony. We naturally recoil with an unmitigated fear, all the while, unable to fight the natural ascent toward our own Via Dolorosa.[33]

The truth is, Floyd rejected Gianna. Rejection may be the worst feeling in the world. All people know it. It doesn't matter how it happens. Whether by a close friend, sibling, or lover, rejection is painful. It disturbs and distorts our senses. Even if we know in our heads that the rejection was baseless and unfair, our emotions cling to it for life. Thus, we are tempted to cuddle and comfort rejection, though it will inevitably invite more inner agony and self-doubt. Rejection, like all painful experiences, must also die.

Also, like any other pain, it too must be grieved. I surmise that much of the backlash of bitterness and vitriol that has come to characterize our culture, may be due to the need to grieve rejection. Though past rejections can be reformulated for a worthy passion or cause, it still needs to be grieved.

Furthermore, we believe deep in our hearts that we are decent, honest human beings—imperfect, yes, but striving to be good people. Rejection challenges this notion and catches us unaware, cutting us to the core. We, quite naturally, try to suppress the pained confusion, and yet to do so, only invites greater loss and damage to our inner selves.

It is worth noting that the pain we feel from a broken heart reportedly is not much different from the pain we

---

33 Via Dolorosa means "the way of grief," "way of sorrow," "way of suffering," or "painful way." The Via Dolorosa is believed to be the path that Jesus walked on His way to his crucifixion.

might feel from a broken arm.[34] Whether physical or emotional, the region of the brain that processes pain is stimulated. In fact, the overlap of physical and emotional pain is so real that when one test group was given acetaminophen as a remedy for the emotional pain, respondents reported feeling much better after a few weeks.[35] Emotional pain is as real as physical pain. With all this in mind, I prayed for Gianna. This would not be easy, but it was necessary.

Gianna entered my office with her newfound optimism, marked by a cheerful bounce in her walk. "Hey Pastor, how are you?"

"I'm great and glad to see you in a positive mood," I replied.

"I feel like I am making great headway with this. Never thought I would make it through six sessions, but each has been so helpful to my progress. I've already told a few friends that you are worth a few listens. So expect some more appointments," Gianna said, smiling.

"I am glad to see you progressing," I replied. "Surely, I don't mind helping anyone work through breakups. But please remember, I'm not a therapist. I'm just helping you think about some issues in light of what a father should have told his daughter. Also, my hope is that these sessions

---

34 Geoff MacDonald, in the chapter entitled "Social Pain and Hurt Feelings", in *The Cambridge Handbook of Personality Psychology*, 2008, editors Philip J. Corr and Gerald Matthews, pg. 542-3. Acetaminophen is a primary drug found in over the counter medications such as Tylenol.
35 Ibid., Pg. 543.

will strengthen your confidence in God. I still need you to seek a therapist to go deeper with your breakup with Floyd. It very well could be a trigger to something deeper in your life. Have you made an appointment with our church therapist?"

"I did, Pastor," Gianna said. "I communicated the same to my friends. They know that they need both. I just want them to know that God is on their side. I just couldn't figure out before where God was in all this. I wasn't ready to abandon my faith or anything, but I couldn't see God in it."

"Well that's cool," I affirmed. "We have extremely gifted therapists who love God and are thoroughly trained in the work of emotional recovery. I can attest, personally, that therapy works. It's a great tool that God uses to help all of us through our darkest and deepest difficulties," I said like I was endorsing the American Association of Psychology.

"Got it Pastor."

"Today, I simply want to know where you are in your healing process with the breakup with Floyd. How long has it been now?" I asked.

"Since the breakup?" Gianna inquired. "Well, we/re in our sixth session, so I'd say about five months?"

"You don't recall the exact day?"

"I do," Gianna said, reluctantly. After a moment, she continued.

"Just trying to put it out of my mind. I'm coming up on six months. It happened on the first Friday of the month. I remember it because that was the day we did our "Friday live" with the Young Adults. I didn't go, though, because of the breakup," Gianna said, now looking down, with another noticeable pause before she uttered the word, "breakup."

"You know, you never told me what happened. Can we talk about it?" I asked.

"I'd rather not," Gianna said after a deep exhale. "But I've learned from you that this is the process." Gianna tried to laugh, but then exhaled again, deeply. I waited patiently until she was ready to speak.

"So, here we go, Pastor," Gianna continued, after nearly a minute. "Funny thing, he was always talking about 'keeping it 100.' But I should have known something was up. There were times when I talked with him that he wasn't his usual self. I would dismiss it as a bad day at work, and kept telling myself it was nothing. So anyway, I should have known something was up, probably did, but I just didn't want to acknowledge it. It's funny, isn't it Pastor? I knew in my heart of hearts before I found out the truth."

"There is a sixth sense about us," I replied. "That first mind has a tendency to tell us something isn't right. It tends to be right more often than wrong. The problem is we don't want to admit t to ourselves, even if it's irrational. So we keep it to ourselves or even totally dismiss it as nothing."

"You're right Pastor. I knew something was up the whole time, but just didn't want to accept it," Gianna said. "So, I had left my iPhone earplugs at his place. I thought I would just drop in and pick them up on my way to the gym. Never made it to the gym of course." Gianna, now, gazing at the floor, as she told her story.

Lifting her head, she continued. "I let myself in his apartment, said 'hi, left my plugs here yesterday,' and headed to his bedroom to get them. He tried to stop me, saying, 'hey G, what's up? I'll get them for you,' not realizing at the time, his tone was really weird. Anyway, by that time, it was too late. I was already at the door of his bedroom, which is when I got that sick weird feeling that someone had been there. The lingering fragrance was a dead giveaway. The crumpled bedsheets on Floyd's bed, also clearly indicated that Floyd was not alone last night—the place where I laid..." Gianna said with stern emphasis, "...listening to him whisper 'love' and 'forevers' in my ear..."

The tears and soft whimper abruptly began. It was an uncontrollable burst. Gianna buried her head into her hands, as she continued to weep. It was not loud as to draw attention to herself; simply a sincere pained weeping. I too felt the anguish of the moment when she discovered the truth. Jesus said, "You shall know the truth and the truth shall set you free." I sometimes wish I can add, "*but the truth hurts, too!*" She was having a good cry, a cry her soul wanted but fought. I just sat in my chair, praying silent. As I inched the Kleenex box closer, I prayed that somehow God's presence would mediate the compassion and hope of Christ. She was now on her cross, much quicker than I had imagined.

As she cried, I couldn't help but think of the Luke 7 woman that came to Jesus.[36] She came in tears, ashamed of her reputation. She was a known woman of the street. Simply put, she sold her body for money. The religious leaders, without a hint of compassion, condemned her without even knowing her name or circumstances. For the record, she had sold her body for money because, like many Jewish women in that day, she had no other means of supporting herself. Many women in the ancient era resorted to prostitution because they did not have husbands or families, the primary and sole income earners of the day, to support them. What would you have done?

Jesus, on the other hand, offered her compassion, forgiveness and grace. Too often, the church is quick to condemn and slow to forgive. Yet, we expect the opposite for ourselves. Moreover, what signifies us as true Christ followers is not the sharp memory of Bible verses, but the capacity to mediate the presence of Christ to others.

Something is deeply wrong if we can experience the presence of Christ personally, but never share the presence of Christ with others in need. Gianna did not need a lecture about how she never should have been in his bedroom. She would eventually learn this lesson. She, however, needed to know Christ was with her, with His care and compassion for her hemorrhaging soul. We all need

---

36 Luke 7:36-50

that hope. As she wiped away her tears with a Kleenex, to my surprise, she was not finished talking.

"You would think that was the worst of it," as Gianna gathered her strength to continue her story. "What wiped me out was when I saw her necklace lying neatly on top of the Floyd's bedside docking station and watch box. I gave him that docking station for Christmas. It's a great piece, in which he can charge his phone and keep up with his wallet, money clip, and keys, since he was always misplacing them. He loved it, because for the first time in his life, he felt organized.

Anyway, I had laid my plugs on top of his docking station, which I often do. When I found my plugs, they were no longer laying across the docking station, but neatly placed on his dresser. In its place, lying on his docking station, was her necklace. It was obvious she had purposefully replaced my plugs with *her* necklace. I didn't need to be a rocket scientist to know that this chick was scandalous. I got the message loud and clear."

Gianna's tears had almost completely dried by now, as she was undergoing a transformation from weeping to anger. I knew it was coming. Pain will do that to you. I have no idea how Jesus remained so calm on that cross.

"In an instant, I noted two things," Gianna said, now feeling her flow. "*First*, this was not a one night stand or a fling. No, this was someone that knew he was in a committed relationship. *Secondly*, that this heifer would purposefully and scandalously replace my plugs with her necklace—

sleeping in my man's bed, like that? Sadly, I don't ever think Floyd knows to this day how low that heifer is. I hope he's happy with her because she's going to do something worst to him!" Gianna's anger was center stage now and it was having its turn.

"So, I turned and looked at him," Gianna continued, "expecting him to say something. He just looked at me speechless. I said to him, 'aren't you going to say something?' He just hung his head and said, 'Gianna.' I am not sure if he said anything after that because I pushed passed him and bolted. I didn't want to hear it. I didn't care. He knew..." All of a sudden, her anger did a disappearing act and agony returned.

"I couldn't even get out the apartment without losing it. The last thing I wanted was that punk to see me in tears, so that made it even worst. It was humiliating," Gianna said, now sobbing softly.

"Okay," I said. She was telling her story, tears, anger, and all. She was in a good flow.

"Have you talked to him since?" I asked.

"He called me," she said, wiping away the few trickle of tears. "Well, thirty-two times to be exact and he texted me about the same number of times. I never answered. It had only been about a week. I didn't want to hear it. Besides, I just think a man ought to talk this out face to face. He knows where I live. He could have come to see me. Fool!" Gianna said, her anger now fighting to retake center stage.

"So, did you eventually talk to him," I pushed further.

"No. He finally stopped calling and texting. Nothing. No texts. No calls. No emails. No notes. No nothing. I havn't heard from him since," Gianna softly sobbing again.

That is what I was after. He never fought for a face to face. Rejection. It is open heart surgery without anesthesia. Cruel, painful, gory—rejection hurts. Gianna has taken two nails.

Painful as this was, however, I couldn't help but smile to myself because Gianna didn't take the bait. Usually in betrayal, the victim's loneliness will drive him or her to do the craziest things. Floyd's decision to cease all attempts at contacting Gianna was, in my opinion, a shrewd play. He stopped pursuing her to let her feel her loneliness; to let her *feel* what she thinks she wants; to let her *feel* what life would be like without him. He was heady. Most people, men included, crumble under the pressure of loneliness. After two or three days, they run back to their lover with tears, pleas and promises, begging for another chance to make it work. They think they are feeling the tug of love, when in fact, they're more feeling the pain of the breakup. Returning to their lover is simply an unconscious attempt to avoid the pain. What's worse, the one who betrayed them bears the feelings and fault of the offender. The ro les are reversed; the classic bait and switch has occurred.

Merciless perpetrators, especially domestic violators, are notorious for playing this game. They are geniuses at leading victims to blame themselves for the perpetrator's abuse. The best decision, under these circumstances, is to wait out the emotions. Ride them out like a rollercoaster. Weather the pain. Hold on to something tight—anything, but the lover! Calm the storm within. It's hard, but it gives one clear thinking, balance, wisdom, and composure. Gianna, to my surprise, made the right decision. She did not chase him, while most do. Like Jesus, she too refused the gall to lessen the pain.

"So, he outright rejected you," I said, flatly. I wanted to make sure she knew the issue at hand. I know it was the third and final nail, but it was necessary.

"I guess that is what you can call it," Gianna replied.

"Do you think..."

Interrupting me before I could finish my question, Gianna finally let it pour. Did it ever pour.

"The fact that, that $%#@ never even tried to talk to me?" dangling her last sentence with a question of incredulity.

"Told me he wanted to marry me," as she yelled. She was feeling it now.

"...and this is how you roll? At least try talk to me face to face! At least be a man about it! At least say, I am worth it! Low down, #$&#. And that heifa...," Gianna trying to catch herself.

"...she better hope I never see her! That b#$% of b#$$%$." Gianna, tried her best to quiet herself. She knew she had said more than she wanted to, but it was what she needed at the moment. I can tell she wanted to apologize for the profanity, yet she clearly knew I understood she meant no disrespect. Besides, this is pain—ugly, grimy, filthy, irreverent, profuse and obscene in all its glory.

Speaking up, I said, "You needed to get that out. It is part of the process. So, you never attempted to contact him?" I asked.

"No, but God, I wanted too," Gianna said, while calming herself. "Told Mom about it. She really had my back and all; like she knew what it felt like. She told me, in no uncertain terms, 'Do not call him! Do not make the first move. He is the offender, thus, he has to come to you.'

Mom was serious, Pastor. I thought she was crazy. And Mom held me accountable—took my cell phone for a few days! Then she made sure I hadn't called or texted him, every day, checking my phone and whereabouts, scoping me out like CIA. It was crazy. But, she was right. I probably would have fallen apart, accepted any old excuse, and given in. Mom wasn't hearing that."

"Wow, your mother really had you. I'm glad you listened to her," I said, approvingly.

"Would be lying if I didn't say it was killing me after the second day," Gianna admitted. "I missed him so much. Thought I was going to vomit a number of times. It is not as bad now, but when it comes—boy, it hurts! I wish it was over! I still miss him. Like I said, I still love him."

Gianna, shaking her head, and softly sobbing. "Don't know what it feels like to be on crack; but getting off of it has to feel like this. Floyd was my crack!" Gianna's last statement bore astonishing insight.

Many poets and songwriters have tried to describe love as a narcotic—intoxicating, exhilarating, or addictive. Helped a wife once through a bizarre divorce.[37] She had been married for 12 years. She thought the marriage was wonderful. One day, she had a conversation with her husband about the future of the family. The next day, he was gone. He never came back. Cut off all contact. No explanation. No warning. No answers. No conversation. Nothing. Just gone. The last time she would hear from him was when he served her the divorce papers a month later. Never heard from him again. She is still in therapy. It's been more than two years, now. She just can't shake him. She would do anything to have him back. No explanation needed. Just come back. Her soul was addicted to him.

"You' re learning a lot. In fact, your mother told you what your father should have told you!" I said this, hoping to lighten the mood.

Gianna cracked a half smile, showing a glimmer of hope. "Give yourself time to grieve the loss," I continued. "But under no circumstances, do not ever try to assuage the pain by reconnecting with him. I know it hurts; but this is the process of healing."

---

37 Actual account and characters are fictitious for the purpose of making the point about the addictive nature of relationships.

Grieving

"Gianna, I pray for you always, but today, I prayed a little extra for you." I said with assurance.

"Thanks Pastor," Gianna replied. "I know somebody has been praying for me. This has really been hard, but I am learning a lot about myself and relationships."

"We got you," I said. "I want to wrap up our time together by looking at Leah and a woman in the book of Lamentations, that I think will be helpful for you. Do you feel up to it or would you rather hit this next time?"

"No, I need to work through this. It's like a hard work-out, only much harder!"

Smiling, I said, "I wouldn't have thought of it that way, but that's a great way to describe it."

"If you recall from our last session," I explained, "we talked about how Leah thought sex would turn Jacob's heart to her. It didn't and it never does. People love because they choose to love, not because we're enticed to love."

"I remember that. Good reminder," Gianna said, nodding.

"Well," I continued, "I think Leah finally realized that only the Lord could love her. Look at this verse in your digital Bible,

> "And she conceived again and bore a son, and said, 'This time I will praise the Lord.' Therefore she called his name Judah. Then she ceased bearing." (Genesis 29:35, ESV)

In the previous instance, Leah believed that children would turn Jacob's heart to her. It didn't. But something happened with the birth of Judah. Apparently, she gave up trying to gain Jacob's love and gave into the Lord. She realized that if this relationship was ever going to be right, she must first trust God."

"This," I explained, "is my hope for you, Gianna. God has a way of moving closer to us in our darkest hour. This is not to say that God doesn't want you to have a healthy loving relationship in your future. It does say that more than anything, the Lord is your strength, your well-being, your blessing. He is the one who can give you a renewed confidence and hope for your future. Trust Him. I hope more than anything today, you feel vitally connected to the Lord and His wonderful plans for your life."

"I didn't think of it like that, but I feel like I am growing stronger. I feel like God is there for me," Gianna said.

"That's great."

"Okay. Gianna, one last thing and we'll be done. Before our next session," I continued, "I want you to read the first chapter of Lamentations for your personal reflection. Lamentations is a book that captures the grief of a nation, during a period of desolation and exile. In Chapter 1, the writer depicts a widow, grieving almost inconsolably, a personal loss. Her grieving is a symbol of how the nation felt over the loss of the city of Jerusalem. It shows us how God's people in those days grieved. There are three things I want you to learn from this story about grief."

~ ~ ~

Grief is a form of protest. "When you read," I explained, "you will feel the sense of protest and injustice expressed by the widow. This is surely what the nation was feeling. It is what you did earlier today."

"Pastor, sorry for the p…"

"No apology needed," I quickly said to prevent her from completing her sentence. "Hear me out. This widow had been faithful to God and now finds herself suffering, immensely. She expresses her grief with anger and protest. That is what you felt today—protest, rage and anger. I know you didn't mean anything by the profanity, but the absence of it would have caused me to pause. My point is, you will naturally feel anger and a sense of injustice as you process this pain."

Grief helps us process emotions. "Grief," I further explained, "is a natural way of processing and making sense of our loss. There are five stages in grief: Denial, anger, bargaining, depression, and acceptance.[38] Now, don't think your emotions operate in a neat sequential order as I have stated. You may feel denial today and acceptance tomorrow, and then depression three days from now. Emotions are tricky with pain. This is just a simple template to help

---

38 Elizabeth Kubler-Ross, *On Death and Dying*, New York: Scribner, 1969), pg. 38, ff, 133-4. Whether tragedy, dying, or death, the process is the same.

you understand your emotional state. In a word, emotions take time to heal. You may experience grief similar to the widow depicted in Lamentations. In order to move beyond a difficult event, your emotions must accept the event as a part of living. That is processing, and it takes time. Your talking to me about what happened to you is a form of accepting what has happened to you, so that you can return to some *normalcy*."

"I encourage people," I continued, "to journal their emotions to further process the events. Have you ever wondered why you are drawn to certain songs?"

Gianna just looked at me as if I should have known her answer.

"Many songwriters," I explained, "write songs to process their personal difficult experiences or issues. The song naturally helps the songwriter, but invariably, helps others.[39] This connection allows expression. Gianna, you need expression. Don't shy away from it. Just as the widow in Lamentations expressed her true feelings to God and others, don't shy away from what you are feeling. Express it and you will process it."

Grief helps us voice confusion toward resolution. "What I mean here," I explained, "is that you will have those moments of confusion that will stump you. One minute,

---

39 Hart, Archibald, *Unlocking the Mystery of your Emotions* (Dallas: Word Publishing, 1979), 11. Dr. Hart remarks that "poets probably do a better job of describing them [emotions]." (Brackets mine)

you will feel like you have grown. The next minute, you will feel like you were set back to square one. This is because, your mind wants a rational explanation for what happened—'Why me? What did I do wrong? Is God angry with me? Am I the problem?' Your mind is trying to rationalize what happened to you. Don't fall for it. It's a trick of the mind. In truth, this is your mind's way of avoiding the pain. The only way through pain is to embrace it emotionally. By accepting it, you heal. Let me say it again, Gianna. *By accepting it, you heal.* This is processing. Every time you simply acknowledge what happened to you as true, you are addressing the pain."

"One of my professors, Dr. Archibald Hart of Fuller Seminary wrote this about healthy emotions: 'The surest sign of maturity is the ability to experience one's emotions freely and integrate them into all aspects of one's being.'[40] That is, just as we experience love and joy, we must be willing to freely experience loss and pain. When we do this, we're able to process the hurt and move forward with a healthy outlook," I said.

I knew I had said a lot, but I wanted Gianna to know the depth of her hurt and that she needed time to grieve, in order to heal.

"That was a lot Pastor," Gianna said, with her keen sense of directness.

---

40 Ibid., ix.

"I know," I replied, "but I want you to know that you are healing and it's a process. Furthermore, I'm not sure we really ever completely recover from a breakup. I think the best that you can do is learn the lesson for your future. So, let this wound be a reminder for your future."

"Spoken like a father," Gianna said with a pointed smile.

Personal and Group Reflection Questions

1) Do you see a parallel between the cross of Jesus and the pain you may bear? Explain. In what ways do you feel God is with you? In what ways do you feel alone?

2) Have you had a betrayal or a hurt similar to Gianna's? What happened? How did you handle it?

3) Have you ever talked to anyone about what happened to you? If so, did you really get it off your chest?

4) Have you grieved your breakups? Your losses? Explain. Do you think there is a place for healthy grieving?

5) What is God saying to you in your hurt and about grief?

Chapter 7

Yes, you need to know when He is ready

"Don't be a woman that needs a man;
be a woman a man needs."

Anonymous

"We are coming to the end of our sessions together, Gianna," I said.

Exhibiting more joy and energy than I could possibly muster in a day, Gianna bounced into my office. "Hello Pastor!" I was not sure how she would bounce back after our last session.

The cross can be horribly cruel. The truth is we are not Jesus. Thank God for that. We don't always have the resurgence of an Easter resurrection. We do rise, however, but sometimes the Saturday before our Easter takes its toll. Even when we rise, the cross rarely leaves us without residuals that are hardly unnoticed.

I am reminded of a favorite story that one of my late mentors was fond of telling. It is a story about a prayer of a preacher. This preacher, while sitting on his front porch one day, saw a small dog wandering down the street. He was not sure if the dog was a stray or lost, but the dog simply was doing what most dogs do—sniffing and searching for food or mischief.

What caught the preacher's attention was how the small dog handled himself while passing by the yard of a large barking Doberman. Ferocity does not begin to describe this large specimen.

"Thank God the Doberman was on a leash," the preacher said to himself. He had yet to witness a pedestrian not react with visible fear, when the Doberman ferociously barked and ran toward the fence. The barking alone would cause one to leap from their skin, and one could only wonder if he might be able to leap the tall fence. Many passed by daily, knowing full well of his barking ritual. Resisting the urge to jump in fright, however, still was an insurmountable feat with this specimen.

This was a daily occurrence for every passerby. Not so for the small dog. Instead, as he passed by the frenzied barking Doberman, he briefly paused in front of the fence. He stared at the fanatically barking Doberman. Then, without even a flinch, he kept going. No dash to safety, no reaction, not even a hint of fear. Only a simple pause and a stare down, and then continuing his sniff and search mission.

After witnessing that event, the preacher prayed this: "Lord, whatever you put in that small dog, would you please put some of it in me?" I, too, have prayed that prayer. Seems to me, Gianna had some of it in her.

"If I had your endless flow of energy, I would have been a millionaire by now," I said with a big smile.

Laughing, Gianna replied, "Only a millionaire? Then one day, I will be a billionaire!"

"Set your sights high, Gianna. Always good to see you. How is your mother?" I asked.

"Good!" Gianna replied. "Told me to tell you that she really appreciates you taking time with me."

Gianna's mother had thanked me a few Sundays ago after the service. I was a bit surprised that she would thank me again. But God knew children needed mothers who simply loved.

"I believe you've made great progress," I shared. "You look like you're feeling much better about yourself. Believe it or not, the moment you feel your best, you can feel better. Therefore, don't ever rest on your best. Instead, keep growing and you will always become better. Better is always better than best."

As with preachers, we occasionally say things that don't make much sense. I couldn't point to one book or source for my mysterious "best" discourse. It sure sounded good, but I must admit, I am still not sure what I said. My goal was simply to encourage Gianna to continue to pursue better.

"Okay Pastor. I know you said something profound. Thanks," Gianna said with a smirk.

"Well, if I confused you, just forget what I said. So how do you think you're doing?" I asked.

"I really feel good Pastor—at least today," Gianna said with good confidence. "I still have my moments. There are times I really miss Floyd, but at least I can say that now without falling to pieces."

"I had an interesting day last week," Gianna continued. "I was in a Starbucks, and not having the best day. It was actually Friday the fifth, six months to the day Floyd and I broke up. So, I thought I would be cool, but it was a little tough. Anyway, I am standing in line at Starbucks, ordering my favorite coffee, a Caramel Macchiato. And this kid is just staring at me. He couldn't have been more than 15, but he kept staring and smiling at me. I thought it was cute, and at first, didn't give much attention to it.

But then he wouldn't stop staring at me! So, after I got my Macchiato, I saw how he and a couple of his friends were whispering and pointing at me. So, you know I had to say something. "So, what's so funny?" I said, which surprised him. He looked embarrassed at first, but then he said, "I'm sorry, but I like your fly Amandla Stenberg T-shirt. She's hot. I just thought it was a little odd that you had a sad face, while she had a big smile." Then he paused and just blurted it out: "Okay, I think you're beautiful!"

His friends pushed him, laughing, as he pushed them back, saying, "I told you I wasn't scared to tell her." I then realized that the Amandla talk was just a gimmick to share his crush on me. I was really touched. I felt that there was something trying to get my attention—*you're still in demand. Don't let Floyd ruin your day.* Smiling, I told the boy, 'if only you were a little older....' and then I walked away. Pastor, I wish you could have seen his blush! I wanted to make his day because he surely made mine," Gianna said with a huge smile.

"Now, that is funny," I said, laughing with her. "So, what did you learn?"

"Well, I felt like God was telling me, it was going to be all right, which is something my father should have told me," Gianna said, while rolling her eyes. I couldn't help but join in with my laughter. My heart was full. Gianna was coming out of it.

She continued. "I learned that I have to press forward each day. I almost lost a good day. Instead, it became another turning point for the positive and a great day for me."

"Cool. What else?" I asked.

"I learned I need to be self-aware. I didn't realize how much my emotions dictate my decisions. Now, I'm much more intentional in my awareness, trying to monitor my moods. I'm beginning to understand why certain things upset me so quickly," Gianna said.

I quickly interjected. "Can you give me one example?"

"I can," Gianna answered. "With Floyd, I didn't speak my mind. For example, though my mother has been the best through all this, we still had our moments. It's good that I'm out on my own and all, but I got to thinking: Why do I push back so hard on my mother, but always went with the flow with Floyd? I also push back with my girls, my boss, ...almost anybody!

But then I realized I was always giving Floyd the benefit of the doubt. I told myself that I was being 'open.' I figured that it was just something men needed. In reality, I was suffocating my true feelings. I wasn't sharing my true self. Even you Pastor, I have not agreed with everything you said, but I really respect you and all, and yet I went with the flow with you too. But, if you were my mother, I would have pushed back like a rabid dog."

"So, what do you really want to say to me?"

"Well, Pastor..." Gianna started, but looked uncomfortable.

"Okay, you don't have to answer that," I quickly said. "I know how it works. I'm just glad you're learning. I just hope it encourages you to speak your mind—even with your Pastor!"

I'm never surprised at the reluctance of people to share their true opinions with a Pastor. It's one of those unspoken codes in the church that says, "He's the man or woman of God." To the contrary, I try to encourage people of faith to "test the spirits," even if I am the main spirit speaking![41]

---

41 I John 4:1.

No one has the corner on a 100% correct interpretation of faith. Surely, we may point you to the right path, but ultimately, we must do our homework and decide for ourselves—prayerfully led by God's Word and Spirit.

"So, why did you do that? Not speak your mind with Floyd?" I asked.

"Well, I don't think it was because I was afraid to lose Floyd," Gianna said emphatically. "I mean, I have strong opinions, but when it came to my..." Gianna paused and shook her head from side to side.

"I just somehow connected loving him with muting my voice for him," Gianna said. "I don't know why. But I noticed that I do that with men I highly respect. I really did respect Floyd; probably too much. So, when he said things about me I sometimes didn't agree with, I just kept my opinion to myself."

"Well," I responded, "I think the people who love us will do everything in their power to draw out our opinions; even the disagreeable ones. Our opinions and values are a reflection of our true selves. Someone who turns a deaf ear to your values, doesn't respect or love you. Remember that in your future relationships."

"Bet." Gianna said.

"Secondly, have you ever written a letter to your dad, telling him exactly how you feel?" I asked.

Gianna looked a little taken aback. But then she said softly, "I haven't. Mind you, I've given him the blues about a few things; but no, not a letter."

"You may want to think and pray about writing your dad a letter," I explained. "You can tell him how you feel, including your relationship with him. This may explain why you struggle to speak your opinions to men. Sometimes, we need to say what we need to say to those that have hurt us the most, in order to say what we want to say to others."

"I can see how that connects," Gianna replied.

"Now, don't think you're going to write this letter overnight or in a week," I said.

"Wouldn't try, Pastor," Gianna responded.

"But you do need to speak your mind," I continued. "Take some time. Write the letter. Get it all out on paper, emotion and all. Say what you been wanting to say. Then let it marinate. Step away from it for a day or two. Then return to it and reread it. Tighten and trim it. Remove all the personal attacks. People shut down on attacks. You want to be heard, not vindicate your hurt. Only God can do that.

Lay out your arguments. Pose your hard questions, with rational support. Then, read it to a close friend who knows you. Ask for their feedback. Then pray over it. Edit it, some more, if needed. Then, and only then, send it with a prayer.

Now, he may never respond. Or, he may respond and never change. Then again, he may change. Regardless, you have made your case. You have told your story. You have shared your heart. It may not solve your issues with your dad, but at least you have shared your opinions with the first man in your life."

Gianna nodded her head affirmatively. "I need to do that Pastor. So much I want to say to him, even though I've already said a lot. I really do think that will help me."

"Great, last question, then I want to share some thoughts with you about future relationships," I said, shifting the conversation.

"Oh Pastor. You don't have to worry about that," Gianna quickly responded. "I am out of the relationship game for a while. I'm focused on getting myself together. It will be some time before I go down that path. Besides, I don't have time for all this foolishness out here."

"Well, you do need time to heal. But you do still have plans for love one day, don't you?" I said with a smile.

"Yes, I do," Gianna said shyly.

"Okay then. File this in your relationship folder so that you can retrieve it at the appropriate time. In the meantime, marinate on it," I said. "Question: What will you do differently in a future relationship?"

After a short pause, Gianna said, "Pastor, that is a good question. I'm just not sure right now."

"Okay. That's cool," I replied. "But before you go into a new relationship, you need to be able to answer that question. A failure to learn from our past is a prescription for a repeat in the future. I don't think you want that, especially since you have come so far."

"Absolutely not. But sometimes, Pastor, if I can be honest..."

"Please....," I responded.

"Am I wrong for wanting to get back with Floyd?" Gianna said, half-pleading. "I hate myself for thinking it, but isn't God forgiving? Don't we serve a second chance God? You are always talking about how God gives us a second, third, fourth, fifth chance—more chances than we can count! You said, 'God purposefully loses count of all the chances He gives us.' Then, why should I keep count of the chances I give Floyd? Shouldn't I give him another chance?"

Gianna somehow had blurted it out. It had been simmering beneath the surface. Her mood changed to a noticeable sadness. The boy at Starbucks was right, that sad face just does not do her justice. Gianna was made for joy, laughter, and energy. My heart ached as I prayed silently for her. She really wants to reconcile with Floyd. This is normal. Love never dies easily.

"I am glad you said it. It's okay. Have you heard from him?" I asked.

"No. Not since his attempts right after the breakup," Gianna replied. "But I know Floyd. He is going to respect my space. He is going to give me my time to heal. He would never want to influence my decision for him. He would want me to make that decision on my own."

"I hear you," I acknowledged. "Clearly, you know Floyd better than I do. I trust that. Your assessment of him may be true. Please hear me today. If this is true, then it will stand up to the test of time. The truth is Gianna, you are still in an emotional recovery state..."

I stopped mid-sentence after I saw Gianna give a noticeable heavy exhale. She tried her best not to roll her eyes, respectfully. It was clear, however, Gianna was not hearing it.

"Okay then. Two things I want you to consider," I said, trying to reconnect with Gianna. "First, only time will determine if these feelings are attachment or true feelings. Many times, especially after breakups, people mistake attachment feelings for true love. They think the feeling is love, when in fact, it is the experience of healing from the emotional amputation.

I know that amputation is a strong word, but that is what we feel in a breakup. The brain center that registers pain from physical or emotional trauma is the same. It's quite possible that you're feeling the pangs and phantom feelings of an emotional amputation. All I'm asking is that you give yourself time to reassess your feelings. They could be love, but are you sure?" I could tell, Gianna did not like the question; but a part of her knew it was true.

"Secondly," I continued, "if you give yourself time to heal, and I mean really heal; and if you and Floyd should attempt to reconcile, at least you will be in a far better position to relate to him. I would rather you be certain on your feelings when attempting to reconcile, rather than unclear and unsure. At least, give yourself time to feel good about yourself, before you try to feel good about someone else."

I could tell by the blank stare and downward tilt of her head that Gianna knew it was the truth. Many ignore my advice and do the very thing I advise against. That is how overwhelming pain can be. Our hearts will do anything to assuage the agony. We will even return to the cross, if we think it will help us. Unfortunately, time is the best therapy.

"Give yourself time?" I said, trying to make eye contact with Gianna. "At least give yourself four more months and see how you feel? You have done five. If you still feel the same way, maybe you can write a letter to him as well. Say all the things you need to say. Then, see where God takes it."

Gianna nodded her head in agreement without looking up at me. I sensed her reluctance.

When A Man is Ready

"Let me share a few thoughts about that next relationship, even if it is Floyd," I said, trying to cheer Gianna up. She mustered a half smile, as she prepared to take notes.

"Shoot," she said. It was business now. No more fun and games. Yet, even a father has to allow his daughter to walk the path she chooses. It's hard, but sometimes, it is the only way to learn.

"Okay," I replied. "Let's return to the relationship of Jacob and Rachel. I want to help you know when a man might be ready for you. It is hard to tell, being a man myself. We are difficult..."

"That is an understatement," Gianna cutting in on my statement.

"Yes, we are," I said. "But here are three questions to keep before you when determining if a man wants you.

"First, *is he willing to invest his energies in your dreams?* "Gianna, this is important," I explained. "A man who loves you will love you more than just for your looks and figure. You know this. But he should cherish your values, your opinions, and your dreams. Look what Jacob does when he meets Rachel for the first time,

> "Now as soon as Jacob saw Rachel the daughter of Laban his mother's brother, and the sheep of Laban his mother's brother, Jacob came near and rolled the stone from the well's mouth and watered the flock of Laban his mother's brother." (Genesis 29:10, ESV)

"Now, that is what I call inspiration," I said. "When Jacob saw Rachel for the first time, he become a superman. He was inspired. Moving that stone from the mouth of the well, was the work of ten men. I like to think that Rachel had an inspiring effect on him. A woman can never make a man, but she can inspire him. Men need that, though we will never admit it."

"But to the point," I continued, "I want you to notice why he moved the stone. Jacob moved the stone so that Rachel could water her flock. Remember, Rachel was a shepherd-ess.[42] Shepherding was her career. So, Jacob showed his

---

42 Genesis 29:9.

love for Rachel by investing energy in what was important to her. A man that loves you will cherish your beauty, values and especially your dreams. If he is the eagle and you are the chicken, something is wrong with the relationship. You, too, were meant to soar. A man who is your boo, is not intimidated with you soaring. As a matter of fact, he will find it inappropriate for him to soar, while you remain on the ground."

"Now, Pastor, that's good," Gianna speaking up. This was the first time Gianna appeared to reengage the conversation.

"Yes," I said, "this is your biggest clue. Is he willing to be the wind beneath your wings? The truth is, in any relationship, both individuals should soar as eagles. At intermittent junctures of the flight, both will have to serve each other as the wind beneath each other's wings. This is what keeps the relationship soaring."

"Agree Pastor," Gianna now clearly reengaged.

"Second, *does he love you with sacrificial love?*" If I seem to be implying a Christian faith here, I am," I said, unapologetically. "There may be no greater way to exemplify the love of the Master, than by loving and serving others as He loved us.[43] Earlier, we noted this about Jacob:

> "Jacob loved Rachel. And he said, "I will serve you seven years for your younger daughter Rachel.""
> (Genesis 29:18, ESV)

---

43 I John 3:16.

The boy was in love," I said.

"Pastor, that is a little too much love for me. I still love Floyd, but I am not going to wait seven years for him!" Gianna said, emphatically.

"Agree," I replied. "All relationships should have limits. But, a closer look at the story will reveal that this is a sacrificial love. He was willing to sacrifice his freedom for Rachel's hand in marriage. Now we hear the phrase, *'sacrifice his life for us'* so often that it has become a cliché. Here is what I take it to mean: *forfeiting what we cherish most for another.* For example, 'I love my Los Angeles Lakers,' I said, with a hearty smile.

"Oh Pastor, must you go there?" Gianna said with a feigned heavy sigh.

"Of course!" I exclaimed. "If I give up an important Laker game for a romantic dinner with my wife, I have expressed sacrificial love to her. Similarly, I want you to ask the questions, 'Is there sacrificial love? Are they willing to forfeit what they cherish for you?'

Third, *do your opinions and values matter?* "Does he really cherish what is important to you?" I continued. "Look once more at Jacob's actions,

"Then Rachel and Leah answered and said to him, 'Is there any portion or inheritance left to us in our father's house? Are we not regarded by him as foreigners? For he has sold us, and he has indeed devoured our money. All the wealth that God has taken away from our father belongs to us and to our children. Now then, whatever God has said to you, do.'" (Genesis 31:14-16, ESV)

This is critical, Gianna. Jacob worked for Laban, Rachel and Leah's father, for thirty years. In those thirty years, Laban cheated Jacob ten times. The tenth time was the last straw. Jacob was done. Now, as the head of his house, he could have simply ordered his wives and household to follow him. He does not. Instead, he had a family meeting with Rachel and Leah, allowing them to voice their opinions. The point is, Jacob valued Rachel's opinion."

"I would not have made it with that polygamy thing!" Gianna stated.

"Noted and agreed," I acknowledged. "Gianna, hear me out. Your opinions and values are a reflection of you—your inner self. That inner self is dying to express herself and be heard. When she is heard, she is whole. Anyone who cannot appreciate your values and opinions, even if they disagree, are not worthy of you. Your opinions and values are yours. Don't silence them—share them," I concluded.

"What if my values or opinions are wrong?" Gianna asked.

"That's okay," I replied. "But you and only you get to decide if they are wrong. Let God or his wisdom convince you of that. Share it with friends and family that you respect or admire. If you trust their insight, let them correct you. In the end, however, you decide if you want to change your opinions and values, not someone else.

Our opinions and values are always changing because we are always evolving. Trust me, I don't see the Lord the same way today as I did thirty years ago. I don't practice my faith the same way today as I did thirty years ago.

Was I wrong back then? Not necessarily. I was growing, evolving, becoming the person God ordained me to become. I see God in a different light today. Our ideas, values, and opinions are always evolving. But only God and our true selves should have the right to change our opinions. No one else. They are your opinions," I said.

"And if I know your mother, she already told you that, didn't she?" I continued.

Gianna, just sat with that signature smile.

Personal and Group Reflection Questions

1) Do you agree that Gianna is progressing in this chapter? Did you learn anything about your personal self-development from her?

_____

_____

_____

_____

_____

2) Are you like Gianna when it comes to your opinion? Are you too opinionated? Or do you tend to mute your opinion for others? Explain.

_____

_____

_____

_____

_____

3) What are the sources of your beliefs and opinions? Are these sources consistent with your faith or what you live out? Explain.

_____

_____

_____

_____

_____

_____

_____

_____

4) Have you ever had desires to return to relationships that you knew were over? How did you handle it?

_____

_____

_____

_____

_____

_____

_____

_____

_____

5) Which question about men connected with you the most? How is God speaking to you about future relationships?

_____

_____

_____

_____

_____

_____

_____

_____

Chapter 8

Yes, you always will need your *Heavenly* Father

"Pray then like this, Our Father,
which are in heaven..."[44]

"So how are you feeling, today?" I asked, as Gianna and I launched into our final session.

Believe it or not, how we feel about ourselves is a reflection of our thinking.[45] Too many people draw the wrong conclusion about their difficulties. In Gianna's breakup with Floyd, for example, one could think that the breakup itself was the root cause of her prolonged sadness, depression,

---

44 Matthew 6:9a
45 Dr. Archibald Hard, *Unlocking the Mysteries Your Emotions* (Dallas: Word Publishing, 1989), 26-32ff.

and hurt feelings. To the contrary, the breakup produced thoughts *or* beliefs about herself, others, and her view of life. Consequently, it was the thoughts and beliefs derived from the breakup that determined the feelings Gianna experienced.[46] Our minds and emotions are wired to operate in unison. So, until we change our thoughts and beliefs, we can rarely change how we feel about ourselves. If Gianna is truly feeling good about herself and her future, it is a great indicator that her thoughts and beliefs are processing the breakup, properly. Thoughts and beliefs to the contrary would produce feelings of low-esteem, self-hatred, or hopelessness. Granted, people sometimes do their best to mask their true feelings. However, a consistent expression of good feelings are hard to replicate. The wisdom writer of the Scriptures was ahead of his time, saying "As a man thinks, so is he..."[47] That is, not the trauma, but our ideas, thoughts, and beliefs resulting from the trauma, determine how we feel. Surely, Gianna is still processing; she is processing, however, in the right direction.

"Pastor, each week is getting better and better," Gianna replied. "All this has caused me to rethink my priorities and future relationships. I have to admit that, at first, I was a bit skeptical about talking to you. Now, I'm so glad I did! I really can see a path forward, now."

"None of this is ever easy," I responded. "It takes great courage to work through a breakup like you have. The goal,

---

46 Ibid., 28-32ff.
47 Proverbs 23:7.

which I think you're hitting every day, is simply to keep pressing forward, day by day, month by month, until the 'new you' fully emerges. Trust me. She is in there (pointing toward her heart). Each day of growth is one step closer to her unveiling, and one day, she'll emerge in full. And if this makes any sense, your 'latter you' will be greater than your 'former you.'"[48]

"That is a great remix Pastor," Gianna said with a chuckle. "I get it."

"Now, let's talk about your walk with God," I said.

Gianna shifted uncomfortably in her chair, as if to suddenly back up. I'm used to it. I leaned in.

"I want to suggest to you that your need for your father is a shadow of a deeper need—for your *Heavenly Father*," I explained. "The parallels are obvious but the experience is hard to grasp." Gianna now, moved into her familiar nodding mode.

"There is a story in John 21," I continued, "that I believe captures the relationship our Heavenly Father desires to have with us. John 21 tells a story about Peter and six of the other disciples who had gone fishing. Jesus had already risen from the grave and had appeared to all of His disciples, including Peter. Peter, if you may recall, had denied the Lord three times.[49] So, this resurrection thing may have been a bit confusing to him. Apparently, it was perplexing for some of the other disciples too.

---

48 Haggai 2:9.
49 Matthew 26:34, Mark 14:30, Luke 22:34

So, Peter and six of the other disciples went fishing, something they enjoyed. My grandmother loved fishing because it helped her think, reflect, or as she would say to, 'clear her mind.' Maybe this is what Peter and the six disciples had in mind—they just needed to clear their heads regarding the resurrection. I've often wondered how long this fishing expedition would have lasted had Jesus not intervened." I continued, "the truth is, once we get away from Jesus, it's so much easier to stay away. The good news is, Jesus showed up to restore His relationship with the disciples, and especially Peter. Look at this verse:

> "Just as day was breaking, Jesus stood on the shore; yet the disciples did not know that it was Jesus. Jesus said to them, "Children, do you have any fish?" They answered him, "No."" (John 21:4-5, ESV)

The word 'children' in this passage, isn't an indication of a parent child relationship between Jesus and His disciples. Instead, it was a common colloquialism, indicating a close friendship. We would use words like 'friend,' 'buddy,' or even 'partner.' Though the disciples had strayed away from Jesus, Jesus still considered them His friends. They had an unbreakable relationship with Jesus, regardless of unexpected events or their behaviors."

I paused to gauge if Gianna was really listening. She was. I resumed. "If there is one word I could give you today Gianna, it would be that Jesus still considers you His *friend*! Hurts can cause us to get away from Jesus. Surely, there is nothing wrong with the need to get away, periodically. We need time to think, reflect, and process our events. However, it becomes very easy to not only get away, but to *stay* away. The good news is, Jesus is still standing on the shoreline of our lives, calling us 'friend'—calling us to himself."

Gianna interrupted. "Pastor," she said, "I haven't done much praying since my breakup with Floyd. Granted, it was not like I was a prayer warrior before I was with him, but I did pray more than I do now.

I'm not mad with God at all: I just haven't had the energy or the desire to pray. I still feel a little disconnected, but deep down inside, I know God loves me. Truth be told, many times, I feel like I'm just going through the motions in church. I'm not sure where I am or what to do."

"Well, you're not alone," I acknowledged. "We all have moments where we would just rather step away. In your case, stepping away may be your way of grieving. A breakup is a loss and all losses require time to grieve. You also could need some time to simply reflect about how these events have affected you or even your view of God. It's in times like these that we tend to see God differently, in a more mature light."

"Pastor, I think that is what I've been doing." Gianna agreed. "I feel I am progressing, but there are times, I'm feeling my way through this—feeling like I'm wading through something, not sure where I'm headed or where God is in all this, if that makes any sense."

Gianna was now delving into the complexity of trauma and pain. Some experts have indicated that there is a double effect with pain.[50] That is, the trauma is twofold—the actual event; and a belated awakening, which I will call for our purposes, the *"aftershock."* That is, one never fully comprehends the wide-ranging impact of initial shock of the actual event and thus, experiences "aftershocks." Thus, reflection and processing is needed in the aftershock recovery, which is the natural way our emotional body heals.

"I hope more than anything, Gianna," I continued, "that you learn something new about God. It really doesn't depend on where you are with God in all this. Remember, Jesus never gave up on Peter and the disciples. Just as Jesus came looking for them, Jesus also comes looking for us; especially when we find ourselves unable to return to Him on our own."

"That's good Pastor. So how do I get back?" Gianna asked.

I had seen that look many times, but this was the first time I saw it in Gianna. Tired, empty, but eager to figure it out, to break the cycle of pain. I call it "the fatigue of the soul." It is like a rubber band that loses its elasticity. Our soul reaches a point where it can no longer "bounce back." Rubber, like any chemical compound, breaks down with time. The break down, however, is accelerated when the rubber is routinely

---

50 Rambo, Shelly. Spirit and Trauma: A Theology of Remaining (p. 7). Westminster John Knox Press. Kindle Edition.

overstretched. It, too, experiences fatigue and becomes worn. Gianna was feeling worn and overstretched. This is another sign that Gianna was progressing.

"Do the same thing I advised you to do with your earthly father," I replied. "Write a letter! Write a letter to your Heavenly Father and tell Him everything you want to tell Him. Be honest! Lay it all out on the table. Don't hide the truth. Don't try to sanitize your words. Simply say what you need to say. If you want to speak reverently, do so. Many speak irreverently. Don't let this surprise you. Trust me, God can handle it. He is waiting for you. Write it."

"I never thought of writing a letter to God. Okay, I'll do it. I feel there are some things *He* should have told me," Gianna said with a little neck action. God surely made sisters unique!

"I hear you," I said, smiling. "You're not the first. Many saints in the Scriptures had issues with God. Jeremiah was a preacher, and he told God that he felt 'tricked' into preaching![51] He also had doubts about how God was running the world. Jeremiah once asked, "Why do the wicked prosper?"[52] Habakkuk, another preacher, questioned God about the innocent people suffering under the evil hand of oppressors.[53] Job had an issue with God regarding his suffering and he surely wasn't pleased with God's silence in

---

51 Jeremiah 20:7.
52 Jeremiah 12:1.
53 Habakkuk 1:13.

the face of unmitigated violence.[54] Even Jesus, our blessed Savior questioned God on the cross, saying, 'My God, my God, why has thou forsaken me?'[55] My point, Gianna, is that God can handle your questions, doubts, and arguments. Usually, these actions are necessary to gain a deeper faith in him."

"I thought that we could never question God," Gianna stated.

"Well, out of reverence, we think we shouldn't." I replied. "God, however, is not looking for automatons. He expects us to use our minds. 'Love the Lord thy God with all thy heart, all thy *mind*....'[56] If we are using the minds that God gave us, then we will naturally have questions.

"I will remember that," Gianna replied.

"In the meantime," I said, "while you're writing that letter to your Heavenly Father, let me prepare you for what your Heavenly Father might tell you in return."

What your Heavenly Father will tell you:

"I love you and am already pleased with you."

"First," I continued, "your Heavenly Father will tell you, 'Gianna, I love you and I am very pleased with you.' He is not pleased with you simply because you are pretty, skilled, or even an achiever, but because He made you.

---

54   Job 10:3; Job 19:7.
55   Mathew 27:46.
56   Matthew 22:37.

"Most mothers love their newborn infant at first sight," I continued, "solely because it's hers. She conceived, nursed, and birthed the newborn. The newborn brought nothing to the relationship to merit its mother's love. The mother, however, loves the newborn unconditionally. Likewise, since God made you, He bears the similar inclination to love you. Like a mother, He is already pleased with you. Do you remember what He said to Jesus at his baptism?"

"I do," Gianna said.

> "and the Holy Spirit descended on him in bodily form, like a dove; and a voice came from heaven, "You are my beloved Son; with you I am well pleased.""
> (Luke 3:22, ESV)

I nodded with her and said, "Gianna, it's very important to note when the Father makes this statement. He didn't say it after the cross; he said it before the cross. There is no record that Jesus had not performed one miracle; Jesus had not cared for one marginalized soul; nor had Jesus preached one sermon. Yet, his father was pleased with him," I explained.

"Gianna, in this performance-driven, approval-hungry, love-starved culture, God already loves you," I stated. "God is already pleased with you, not because of what you have done, but because of who you are. You don't have to bargain with God to get what you want. You don't have to ramp up your religious energy and language to get God to love you. He loves you and is pleased with you right now, unconditionally."

"This also means," I continued, "that since God made you, he values you. Value is not something we wish, hope, or earn from God, it has already been bestowed. God values us because we are made in his image, which means there is nothing on this earth that compares to our value.[57] Furthermore, there is nothing on this earth that can give us value—no parent, friend, achievement, amount of money and surely no man. Our value is inherent and eternal. God has bestowed upon us an eternal worth. We must embrace this value in ourselves. Your greatest next step of growth may simply be to value yourself the way your Heavenly Father values you. This value gives us meaning and teaches us how to value others."

"So you see, Gianna, rejection does not tarnish our value," I explained. "This is a hard truth to grasp. The Father knew the rejection awaiting Jesus. Thus, the Father prepares him for the inevitable rejection—you already have value. Don't forget that. This is why our walk with God is so important. In our daily walk, our Heavenly Father affirms us even in the face of rejection. Difficulty and opposition are opportunities that our Heavenly Father uses to remind us of our

---

57 Genesis 1:26, 5:1-2, Romans 8:29, I Corinthians 11:7, 2 Corinthians 3:18, Colossians 3:10. Though the image of God has been marred by sin, as followers of Jesus, we are recreated and being refashioned into his glorious image. We all bear the image of God in the sense that God made all human beings, which is called the teaching of *Imago Dei*. Though this image has been marred by sin, it is restored in Christ, which signifies that we are indeed God's own.

value. Gianna, I'll say it again—your big next step may be to embrace God's value of you. Rejection can *never* tarnish your value. Your value is constant, fixed, and eternal, regardless of the times."

Gianna, shifted in her chair, clearly absorbing my sermonette.

"I have a purpose for you"

"Second," I continued, "your Heavenly Father will tell you that your greatest pain pales in comparison to your greater purpose. Listen to what Jesus said about his father, when he was arrested,

> "Do you think that I cannot appeal to my Father, and he will at once send me more than twelve legions of angels? But how then should the Scriptures be fulfilled, that it must be so?" (Matthew 26:53-54, ESV)

"This is an interesting statement," I said. "Jesus could have chosen a detour to the cross. Calling down twelve legions of angels would have ended the charade. Given that a legion of Roman soldiers was about 5,000 men, Jesus could have called down 60,000 angels to defend him. Instead, Jesus chose the cross. Why? Because Jesus knew that the cross wasn't just God's punishment, but more, God's path toward a greater purpose."

"Gianna," I explained, "the greatest mistake people make regarding difficulty is to assume that pain is punishment from God. Many people of faith, and even non-faith, are angry with God because of the painful events that have transpired in their lives. Granted, I don't intend to minimize or even trivialize anyone's pain. Pain is never fun and has a profoundly damaging effect on us all. It, also, can cause us to raise questions about God, his existence, and the meaning of life. However, sometimes the pain is the path toward greater meaning. I believe this is the message of the cross for us today: God can birth a greater purpose out of our greatest pain."

"That's deep, Pastor," Gianna said.

"People don't realize," I continued, "that the gospel was never designed to insulate us from pain. Too many Christians misconstrue Christianity as a problem-free or pain-free faith. To the contrary, the majesty of the gospel inspires us to confront our greatest pain and transform it into an even greater purpose. Of course, this sounds better than it feels! As you walk the path of life with Him, you'll discover a far greater purpose for living. The very pain we suffer might be the door to our greater purpose. Only God can miraculously transform the *greatest tragedy into your greatest triumph.*"

Gianna adjusted herself firmly in her seat, clearly pondering my talk.

"I hate what happened to you," I continued. "It was unfair and unfortunate. It's a scar that will remain with you. You have to decide, however, if the scar will be a wound or a testimony. A wound never heals, reminding you of the past and blocking your forward motion. A testimony, on the other hand, offers hope, transforming the injury into a launching pad toward a purpose. Please don't mistake your pain as rejection or even punishment. It is a path. There is a path toward a greater purpose that your Heavenly Father has for you," I concluded.

"Now, that is something my father should have told me," Gianna quipped, bringing levity to our conversation.

"He should have," I agreed.

"I have good gifts for you"

"Lastly, I believe your Heavenly Father will tell you, 'I have good gifts for you,'" I said. "Listen to this scripture,

'Every good gift and every perfect gift is from above, coming down from the Father of lights, with whom there is no variation or shadow due to change.' (James 1:17, ESV)

This is vitally important to grasp. God, your Father, only gives good gifts! Will you let that sink in for a moment?"

"Hmm. I think I know where you are headed," Gianna replied.

"Let me ask you a question: Why do people repeatedly choose bad relationships?"

Without the slightest hesitation, Gianna blurted, "it's how they see themselves. They think this is the best it's ever going to get!"

"Exactly," I said. "It's a reflection of how they value themselves. People make bad decisions out of their own sense of tarnished value. Therefore, people think that they deserve bad gifts. Just think about what we eat when we are in a bad mood—ice cream, cupcakes, and all the wrong foods, and..."

"...and Snicker bars, Cheetos, and buying clothes we know we can't afford...", Gianna interjected.

"...and the list goes on," I said. "We all do it, don't we?"

"Yes," Gianna said with a huge exhale, nodding her head in agreement.

"If we truly believe we have value from above," I continued, "if we believe our Father values us and bestows only good gifts, then we will naturally chose the *best* gifts for ourselves. Thus, we must trust our Heavenly Father for the good gifts that he gives to us, whom he dearly loves.

"Please remember this Gianna, you are a very good gift," I said with finality. "Therefore, your Heavenly Father only gives you good gifts. When you write your letter to your Heavenly Father, lay everything out on the table. When it's all said and done, your Heavenly Father will say: 'You are a *good gift*. I only have good gifts for you.'

"I can't wait to hear my Daddy say that!" Gianna exclaimed.

Personal and Group Reflection Questions

1) Do you think Gianna's issues were connected to her father? Explain.

_____

_____

_____

_____

_____

_____

2) Describe your relationship with your father. Is it good or bad? Was it the primary relationship that prepared you for life? Explain.

_____

_____

_____

_____

_____

_____

3) Do you have a relationship with God?[58] (Please read footnote) If not, why not? If you do, how has it helped you personally?

_____

_____

_____

_____

_____

4) Which principle about your Heavenly Father encouraged you? Explain.

_____

_____

_____

_____

---

58 If you know Christ, I can confidently say that whatever issue this book has addressed, God is using it to draw you closer to him. He is your Heavenly Father and wants a personal relationship with you. If you do not know Christ, I want to encourage you to consider trusting Christ. The gospel is ten simple words, **[Christ died for our sins and rose from the dead—Bolded for emphasis only]** (John 3:16, Romans 6:23, 10:10) If you believe this, God will save you and give you abundant life (John 10:10). It's the best decision you will ever make.

5) What is God saying to you about your relationship with Him, yourself, and your future love relationships?

.

Epilogue

"Whatever you do, _work_ heartily,
as for the Lord and not for men,"
~ (Colossians 3:23, English Standard Version, Underscore mine) ~

I wrote this book to give women a fatherly perspective on disappointments, relationships, and personal wholeness. I wrote it in the form of a fictional narrative to help readers better capture the "feeling" of these issues. Gianna's story was a means of accomplishing this purpose.

Gianna is not a real person nor were any actual stories utilized for this book. Just as Jesus told parables—made up stories to illustrate a truth—so also, I made up Gianna and her story. While neither she nor her stories are real, her hurts _illustrate_ truth: Loneliness, betrayal, and rejection feel real. Whether in a parable or a true story, hurts, betrayals, and disappointments feel real and touch us in a personal way because we relate to them from our personal experiences.

Mother Teresa may have said it best when she said: "Loneliness and the feeling of being unwanted is the most terrible poverty." Experiences of rejection and betrayal can produce feelings of an almost unbearable loneliness and an unwanted poverty of the soul. Something feels missing and we can feel isolated in a way no one else understands.

These experiences also can have an adverse effect on how we feel about ourselves and how we engage other relationships. My prayer for you is that this book was a mechanism to connect and express your personal experiences through the lens of Gianna's story. Acknowledging these experiences, in my opinion, is the first and perhaps the most critical step toward wholeness.

My father is fond of saying this: "The only place success comes before work is in the dictionary." He said it so often that my younger son quoted him on a college application essay! (He was accepted into the school)

I must admit that I didn't get the point of my father's proverb until I reached adulthood. Since then, however, I have found the statement to be profoundly true in just about everything in life. *Success at anything requires work.* Whether career, marriage, parenting, personal goals, or yes, life hurts such as Gianna's, it all requires work.

We understand this, intuitively, but somehow we still seem to hope for a different outcome; that somehow, we'll be the exception to this rule. For Christians, we even try to pray the hurt away as though Jesus will just snap his Divine "fingers" and all will be instantaneously well.

Life doesn't work that way. If we want a healthy recovery from our hurts; if want to experience a blossoming of maturity and wholeness, we must put in the work. And, if we put in the work, I believe God, not only enters our recovery process as a comforting and supportive presence, but also sends wonderful caring and gifted people to help us along the way.

By work, I do not mean that we work with an obsessive compulsion for perfection in our inner selves. Most assuredly, life is full brokenness and we are almost guaranteed to encounter future hurts. We all bear a measure of brokenness, whether from life hurts, our imperfections, or trying to make life work in a broken world. We may never "arrive" at a destination of ultimate wholeness, but we definitely can "grow" toward it.

Knowing that a better version of ourselves always is emerging, in my opinion, *is* the refreshing experience of wholeness. Personal growth is wholeness. Every step of development is a step in wholeness. With each step, we all are reminded that we are fearfully and wonderfully made; each stamped with an unmistakable and meaningful purpose. We discover that we are made for healthy relationships and we indeed, can gain the courage and capacity to share and receive love.

As we grow, we must be careful not to succumb to temporary substitutes or solutions for our hurts. When we are hurting, we are tempted to find an "anesthesia" to deaden the pain. Unfortunately, in time, the anesthesia wears off and the pain returns. We become even more disappointed and may feel betrayal because our temporary substitute or solution did not deliver the love and recovery our hearts needed.

The Christian worldview calls these substitutes and solutions, "idols." Idols may sound silly to the 21st century ear, but no matter how advanced we are, we all have them, and must continually fight to displace them. Tim Keller provides a modern definition of an idol in this manner:

> "It is anything more important to you than God, anything that absorbs your heart and imagination more than God, anything you seek to give you what only God can give...If anything becomes more fundamental than God to your happiness, meaning in life, and identity, then it is an idol."[59]

Therefore, idols are more than graven images people venerate. Idols can be anything or anybody. We can make idols of friends, relatives, or lovers; money, status, and a desire for fame. We can make idols of addictions or dysfunctional behaviors that only invite more shame. If we are not careful, idols can consume us.

---

59 Keller, Tim. *Counterfeit Gods: The Empty Promises of Money, Sex, and Power, and the Only Hope that Matters* (New York: Penguin Group, 2009), Kindle location 133 and 147,

Idols can even give us a false sense of self, an illusion that we are getting better, when in reality, we are only getting worse. When our idols crumble, reality hits. We crash with a feeling worse than the initial experience of disappointment. We must be mindful that pain tempts us to seek out idols, but they are only temporary remedies for long-term solutions.

To avoid the trap of idols, it often is best to seek out a therapist or counselor. Too often, we have been taught in our faith traditions to simply "go to church, pray and the Lord will heal you." Meanwhile, God has provided professionally-trained and spiritually-gifted people who can assist us with our healing.

I am not suggesting that God cannot heal all by Himself. God often uses people as His agents of healing and provides resources and people who are skilled to help us in our recovery. We understand this when we go to a physician for physical sickness and ailments. The same holds true for ailments of the heart, mind, and soul. The church is filled with gifted and trained people, who serve their communities with counseling. Take advantage of it. Go see a professional. It's okay to see someone trained in therapy. My wife and I have gone to a counselor together, and we each have seen counselors, individually. Moreover, every year, I see a counselor just to assess how I am doing. Shed the fear and do yourself a favor: Go to counseling.

My final thought for you is this: *Don't run from your hurts or pains; instead, embrace them!* You never need to be ashamed of the hurts you have endured. Never hide from your difficulties; instead, confront them. Never shrink from your disappointments; instead, grow through them. God will bring you through if you allow him to walk with you. You will experience growth and wholeness. This path *always* will produce a better you! You will learn more about yourself and, most importantly, about the God who loves you.

This has been my aim in life and I pray that it will become yours. This is the message of the cross, the message I believe and live by: Even in our greatest tragedy, God will give us an even greater triumph.

I pray God's best for you and leave you with two of my favorite quotes that guide me toward a satisfied life. Blessings and great relationships to you.

"The unexamined life is not worth living."
~ Socrates ~

"Let a man regard us in this manner,
as servants of Christ..."
~ (I Corinthians 4:1a) ~

Made in the USA
Columbia, SC
03 March 2020